Praise for *The Shaping of Thought*

"I think this book would be excellent as a supplemental text for undergraduate methods classes in reading, but also in content-area reading classes. We also have a beginning master's course in which the book would be very appropriate. . . . While I have read a few books on this topic over the years, I think the strength of *The Shaping of Thought* is in the depth of treatment of the topic. Teachers who use this book will surely appreciate the development of metacognition and higher-level thinking."

—**Linda B. Gambrell**, PhD, distinguished professor of education, Clemson University

"I found this effort to be educationally sound, aesthetically appealing, and user friendly. It should become an invaluable resource for both teachers and administrators. Its most promising attribute may be the amount of assistance provided for teachers in helping students understand, refine, and appreciate thought processes. This critical teaching is prominent among those that are becoming essential to the teacher evaluation process."

—**Thomas Brown**, EdM, elementary principal (retired); author and consultant in urban education

"This was a book that needed to be written. . . . *The Shaping of Thought* is an excellent guide that provides instructional tools for teachers . . . to help students organize their thoughts in response to literature. . . . I have observed the success . . . of ThinkLinks with all grades at the elementary level. . . . Teachers were able to help students achieve higher levels of understanding. Students were able to communicate their thoughts from their readings, utilize them in guided teacher discussions, and, finally, produce their ideas in written tasks. Reading and writing skills improved. Additionally, I have seen some of these strategies work effectively with students with special needs. . . . The authors are extremely talented people, and I felt honored to work with them."

—**Leah M. Farmer**, EdM, elementary principal (retired); key administrator in the teacher education center collaboration between the University of Maryland and Howard County, Maryland, schools

"One of the strongest components of the book is how you discuss thinking and metacognition and then show concrete examples of a nontangible thought process. To me, this blend of theory with specific, concrete student responses is also what distinguishes this book from others that discuss metacognition or visual organizers. The inclusion of student examples for each and every ThinkLinks step is a strong advantage of this book over others. . . . For critical, even skeptical, educators who want proof of the benefit of using these teaching strategies, the actual student responses should be ample proof of effectiveness."

—**Marianne Sane Pfeiffer**, PhD, elementary school principal (retired)

"Over the years these authors have struggled with, sketched, shaped, sculpted, synergized, and now solidified *The Shaping of Thought*. The collection of varied links is dazzling, and the kaleidoscope list is truly transformational. Congratulations on this impressive achievement."

—**Neil Davidson**, president of Cooperative Learning International; formerly mathematics professor at the University of Maryland, College Park

"*The Shaping of Thought* helps teachers and students focus on the use of mapping to promote the organization of ideas and further thinking—hence the term 'ThinkLinks' that stress purpose and focus. . . . [The book] connects the use of these to writing tasks and hints at the power of talk. . . . Good to see ThinkTrix as a foundation . . . as it can trigger useful questions for teachers and students."

—**John Myers**, professor, University of Toronto

The Shaping of Thought

A Teacher's Guide to Metacognitive Mapping and Critical Thinking in Response to Literature

Frank T. Lyman Jr., Charlene López, and Arlene Mindus

ROWMAN & LITTLEFIELD
Lanham • Boulder • New York • London

Published by Rowman & Littlefield
A wholly owned subsidiary of The Rowman & Littlefield Publishing Group, Inc.
4501 Forbes Boulevard, Suite 200, Lanham, Maryland 20706
www.rowman.com

Unit A, Whitacre Mews, 26-34 Stannary Street, London SE11 4AB

British Library Cataloguing in Publication Information Available

Library of Congress Cataloging-in-Publication Data Available
Names: Lyman, Frank T., Jr., author. | López, Charlene 1940– author. | Mindus, Arlene, 1943– author.
Title: The shaping of thought : a teacher's guide to metacognitive mapping and critical thinking in response to literature / Frank T. Lyman Jr., Charlene López, and Arlene Mindus.
Description: Lanham : Rowman & Littlefield, [2017] | Includes bibliographical references.
Identifiers: LCCN 2016030861 (print) | LCCN 2016045271 (ebook) | ISBN 9781475830316 (cloth : alk. paper) | ISBN 9781475830323 (pbk. : alk. paper) | ISBN 9781475830330 (electronic)
Subjects: LCSH: Reading comprehension—Study and teaching (Elementary) | Critical thinking—Study and teaching (Elementary) | Reading, Psychology of. | Metacognition in children. | Cognitive maps (Psychology)
Classification: LCC LB1050.45 .L95 2017 (print) | LCC LB1050.45 (ebook) | DDC 372.47—dc23
LC record available at https://lccn.loc.gov/2016030861

♾™ The paper used in this publication meets the minimum requirements of American National Standard for Information Sciences—Permanence of Paper for Printed Library Materials, ANSI/NISO Z39.48-1992.

Printed in the United States of America

Coauthors Frank and Arlene dedicate this book to coauthor Charlene López, whose long, successful career in education, style of teaching, and determination that all children think deeply about literature and life are firmly embedded in this book.

Contents

Foreword

Today's educators face exhortations to employ "research-validated" teaching strategies so as not to leave any child behind. While the proposition is sound, the devil resides in the details. Indeed, there are literally thousands of "how to" publications promising the latest and greatest in such pedagogical solutions as brain-based learning, differentiated instruction, formative assessment, multiple intelligences, English language learning, critical/creative thinking, cooperative learning, portfolios, graphic organizers, energizers, and summarizers.

Moreover, a veritable cottage industry has flooded the market with "test prep" resources promising to raise scores on high-stakes state and national accountability tests. How can dedicated educators ever sort through the plethora of instructional support materials to find the ones that will truly enhance student learning? I suggest employing two primary criteria for judging teaching techniques and related instructional materials:

1. Demonstrated effectiveness over time
2. Practical and feasible for today's overworked teachers

Created and refined as a result of more than forty years of classroom experience and accompanying research, ThinkLinks unequivocally meet the first criterion. Recent evidence of their efficacy comes from the meta-analyses conducted by noted educational researchers, Dr. Robert Marzano[1] and John Hattie,[2] who highlight the value of compare/contrast, nonlinguistic representation, cooperative learning, and metacognition—all integral parts of using the ThinkLinks.

Further support for the ideas in *The Shaping of Thought: A Teacher's Guide to Metacognitive Mapping and Critical Thinking in Response to Literature* comes from the field of neuroscience. Dr. Judy Willis,[3] a neurologist and teacher, describes the many positive neurological effects of using graphic organizers across the curriculum to assist students in processing information, storing knowledge in long-term memory, seeing new patterns, and reflecting on their learning.

As for the second criterion—the ThinkLinks visual organizers are eminently practical and easily applied by beginning and veteran teachers alike. Although straightforward in concept, ThinkLinks are not simplistic. They allow learners to explore and communicate multiple layers of meaning without artificially constraining thinking, as do many prepackaged graphic organizers. Indeed, the book's title, *The Shaping of Thought: A Teacher's Guide to Metacognitive Mapping and Critical Thinking in Response to Literature*, aptly describes the use of ThinkLinks to make the "invisible visible."

A unique aspect of the book involves the linking of the ThinkTrix thinking framework with associated visual generation and organization of thought. Years of classroom use, dozens of teacher testimonials, and hundreds of student creations attest to the power and effect of the ThinkTrix strategy.

Your teaching will blossom as a result of this book and your learners will benefit from the resulting fruits.

Jay McTighe

NOTES

1. Marzano, Robert, J., et al. (2001). *Classroom Instruction that Works.* Alexandria, VA: Association for Supervision and Curriculum Development.

2. Hattie, John. (2009). *Visible Learning: A Synthesis of Over 800 Meta-Analyses Relating to Achievement.* New York, NY: Routledge.

3. Willis, Judy, M.D. (2008). *Teaching the Brain to Read: Strategies for Improving Fluency, Vocabulary, and Comprehension.* Alexandria, VA: Association for Supervision and Curriculum Development.

Preface

The Shaping of Thought: A Teacher's Guide to Metacognitive Mapping and Critical Thinking in Response to Literature, contains visual organizers, as well as the highest levels of their development, as a vehicle to help students gain an in-depth understanding of literature and thus themselves. It gives a comprehensive look at **ThinkLinks,** a student-friendly name for cognitive maps, or visual organizers.

The approach to metacognitive mapping in this book was discovered serendipitously by Dr. Frank Lyman in 1965 at Estabrook Elementary School in Lexington, Massachusetts, and developed by teacher colleagues and graduate students in Maryland beginning in 1968. These teachers were predominantly Howard County teachers, several of whom, such as Charlene López and Arlene Mindus, gave the students full rein to invent and use a variety of **ThinkLink** shapes. Though cognitive mapping has been developed, replicated, and researched nationally and worldwide in other settings since 1970, the **ThinkLink** metacognitive mapping strategy has features uncommon to other variations. The central concept is that all thought can be shaped, or designed visually, and that each thought can have more than one inventive and representative design. Secondly, every thought or question/response consists of one or more fundamental actions of the mind. The **ThinkTrix**, as a fundamental thinking typology, consists of seven symbols, or icons, that represent these mind actions, or types of thinking, and hence acts as a kind of Rosetta Stone translator for the multitude of terms used to describe thinking. Each **ThinkLink**, or metacognitive map, is made up of some combination of the basic mind actions from the **ThinkTrix**. This metacognitive framework can be used to ask and answer questions and design thought shapes, or **ThinkLinks**. By understanding and revealing the architecture of thought, the teacher renders reading, writing, and thinking more accessible to students.

A teacher who pays close attention to the contents of *The Shaping of Thought: A Teacher's Guide to Metacognitive Mapping and Critical Thinking in Response to Literature* will be rewarded with a deeper sense of learning and how to develop true understanding in the classroom.

ThinkLink Prototype Shapes

ThinkLink Prototype Shapes

All thought has shape. The shapes shown here are only a fraction of the possibilities.
Many of these have been invented by elementary students, who are extraordinarily able to create
them when challenged to do so. They are often added to and placed on display around the walls.

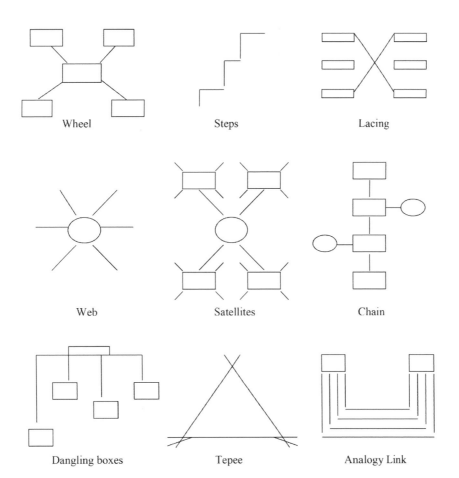

Wheel   Steps   Lacing

Web   Satellites   Chain

Dangling boxes   Tepee   Analogy Link

ThinkLink Prototype Shapes (*Continued*)

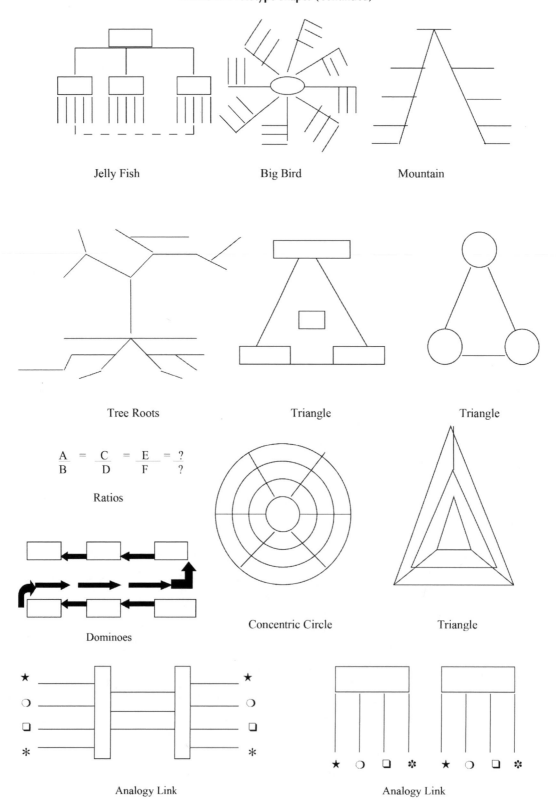

Jelly Fish

Big Bird

Mountain

Tree Roots

Triangle

Triangle

$$\frac{A}{B} = \frac{C}{D} = \frac{E}{F} = \frac{?}{?}$$

Ratios

Dominoes

Concentric Circle

Triangle

Analogy Link

Analogy Link

Acknowledgments

The authors would like to acknowledge the contributions of the following teachers, facilitators, supervisors, and administrators to the development of the ThinkLink Classroom with the ThinkTrix component: Shirley Rogers Newman, Belinda Miller, Nancy Koza, Thommie DePinto Piercy, Joanne Soporowski, Teresa Bridger, Pat McTighe, Sam Polack, Tom Bruner, Monica Diaz Palumbo, Hema Kumar, Darlene Sabelhaus, Sharon Vargo Olson, Chips Merkle, Leah Farmer, Karen Arick, Anne Eustis, Ann Mintz, Larry March, Tom Payne, Barbara Garnes, Sharon Giorgio, Dorothy Burrus, Bobbie Fagan, James Pope, Toni Worsham, Marianne Pfeiffer, Tom Brown, Kathy Prince, Pam Fields, Dorothy Chidester, Terese Verchinski, Ellen Weiss, Amy Dower, Sharon Laurich, Carol Phillips, Tamera Sherr, Barbara Allen, Lauri Edinger, Norman Marceron, Molly Ketterer, Bill Ferguson, Kim Flyr, Debbie Wolf, Rickie Richardson, Carla Beachy, Leah Amato, Mary McKnight, Francis Baranson, Paige McGee, Karen Curtin Atabeck, Linda Brown, Thomas Cole, Pat Richardson, Debbie Klein, Kathy Ryan, Susan Solomon Shetzig, Laurie Ann Parietti Harvey, Dianne Hoffman, Sharon Craig, Janice Knight, Mychael Willon, Rose Levine, Karen and Steve Silverman, Carolyn Adger, Molly Flender, Kathy Glaser, Colleen O'Donnell, Doris Roettger-Svoboda, Allen Irvine, Shirley Kellam Vie, Marie D'Angelis, Carol Williamson, Joan Coley, Jeanne Dussault, Kayda Cushman, Jane Irving Bond, Pat Wilson, Sue Winkler, Rae Ann Wuestman, Nancy Holmwood, Treva Hilliard, Susan Tyrie Schmelz, Wendy Matthews, Emily Vissers, Lisa Caplan, Debbie West, James Wagner, Mary Nimmich, Gail Donahue, Kathy Kreidler, Mary Ellen Doyle, Jane Lagioia, Kathleen Carroll, Doris Vanek Novak, Kathy Carroll, Barbara Hoffman, Jay McTighe, John Thomas, and Joseph Grannis.

We would like to thank Spencer Kagan and Miguel Kagan for their support throughout the years and for disseminating Think-Pair-Share and ThinkTrix to a wider audience.

University of Maryland professors Robert Wilson, Linda Gambrell, Barbara Kapunis, Pat Koskinen, Beth Davey, and John Madison deserve special note for their efforts in promoting research on the ThinkLink metacognitive mapping strategy. Joyce Murphy, Evelyn DiTosto, Richard Arends, Lenore Cohen, Jay McTighe, and Lee Smith also promoted the development and practice of ThinkLinks and ThinkTrix.

Thanks also to staff developers in Howard, Carroll, Baltimore, Ann Arundel, and Prince Georges Counties' Public School Systems.

Special recognition goes to James Moffett for inspiring, accepting, and sharing several of the ideas included in the ThinkLink Classroom.

The preparation of this book was made possible by the skilled efforts of Eleanor Jose, Carroll Yingling, Rudy López, Sharon Vargo Olson, and Suzanne Green.

We would like to express our sincere gratitude to Michael Aslett, Jacqueline Flamm, and Megan Kellerman for their initial efforts in publishing our book. We also wish to thank Sarah Jubar and the staff at Rowman & Littlefield for their interest and support in publishing this book.

Introduction

Definition

ThinkLinks are cognitive maps that enable students and teachers to generate ideas and find relationships. **ThinkLinks** are a metacognitive mapping strategy of creation and connection and are based on the premise that all thought can be shaped and that thought itself can be understood. This book describes some uses of **ThinkLinks** as tools for oral and written response to reading, as well as the use of the **ThinkTrix** typology to help students understand how they think. This strategic combining of the seven **thinking types** of the **ThinkTrix** typology with the cognitive mapping of the **ThinkLinks** is a key route to reading comprehension and understanding of literature and is crucial for maximum student engagement in learning.

Applicability

ThinkLinks are used at any grade level, with learners of any ability, and with any subject matter. **ThinkLinks** and the way they are taught differ according to the situation and the **type** of thinking required. The **ThinkLink** metacognitive mapping strategy has two basic uses: to generate new knowledge, as when a concept or generalization is derived from concrete examples, and to organize previous knowledge, as happens when example is connected to concept or generalization.

Students use the **ThinkLink** to respond to fiction, nonfiction, or to personal experience. Using the **ThinkLink** as a medium, they recall events or events in sequence, infer cause and effect, analyze characters, make comparisons, and derive or exemplify themes and concepts. The **ThinkLinks** are constructed in many shapes, or **forms**, and can be uniquely designed and artistically embellished. Student invention of the shapes is a major element.

A **ThinkLink** can be used as a metacognitive map, as a learning experience in itself. This end product **ThinkLink** is often a result of discussion and can also be used as a focus for further discussion. Some teachers use the students' maps as a source of evaluative information to share with students and their parents the quality of the students' thinking. The point is that, as an end product, **ThinkLinks** can be valuable in facilitating thinking.

One problem in achieving an orderly written or oral expression of knowledge is the difficulty of preliminary organization. Points of view, reporting, or research rarely emerge full-blown in written form. An intermediate step between what is in the mind and final expression on paper can be a graphic pattern, a thought design in which parts and whole, cause and effect, concept and example, and example to example, are linked in relationship. Such a design, or a **ThinkLink**, as it is generically referred to here, is a **blueprint** for written or oral expression. In other words, it can be used as a content organizer from which to craft a coherent piece of writing or speaking.

The Framework

The metacognitive framework of **ThinkLinks** for literature and reading is best visualized as a matrix with one axis being the departure points, or focal points, and the other axis being the seven basic **thinking types** involved. The modified matrix, or **ThinkTrix**, below includes six thinking **types** and four departure points, and is useful as an organizer for this book. The more complete version of the **ThinkTrix** for classroom use has more departure points and seven thinking types, as shown on page 6.

Modified ThinkTrix

Thinking Types	Character 1	Event 2	Theme 3	Story 4
R Recall · a	1a	2a	3a	4a
Cause ↔ Effect · b	1b	2b	3b	4b
Similarity · c	1c	2c	3c	4c
Difference · d	1d	2d	3d	4d
💡 → Ex · Idea → Example(s) · e	1e	2e	3e	4e
Ex → 💡 · Example(s) → Idea(s) · f	1f	2f	3f	4f

Every **ThinkLink** shown in this book begins with character, event, theme, or story and contains one or more of six basic thinking **types**. The categorization of **kind** refers to the starting point of the thinking. This metacognitive classifying scheme, as shown on pages 2, 6, and 7 for the thinking **types**, was derived by the authors from hundreds of student-constructed **ThinkLink** samples; hence, its validity and practical value to teacher and students.

Throughout the book, one or more of the grid cell codes, shown in the modified matrix above, identifies the thinking involved in the **ThinkLink** prototypes and samples. Properly understood and often used together with a number of different **ThinkLink** shapes, or **forms**, the **ThinkTrix** becomes a clarifying metacognitive tool for teacher and students to create, analyze, and respond to questions. Metacognitive mapping is the combination of **ThinkLinks** and the seven thinking **types** of the **ThinkTrix**, as seen in pages 2, 6, and 7.

Uses of the Book

The purpose of this book is to give the teacher of reading and literature the benefit of fifty years of **ThinkLink** field-testing. The teacher should be able to grasp the essence of the **ThinkLink** metacognitive mapping strategy and make effective use of it by reading this text and considering the various prototypes and samples, as well as the thinking that underlies them. The reader may refer to the literature and research on cognitive mapping for justification and for variations by other names.

The book chapters, **Character**, **Event**, **Theme**, and **Story**, representing **kinds** of **ThinkLinks**, are divided into explanatory and instructional sections. As described in the first chapter on Character ThinkLinks, the instructional strategy has two stages: *Demonstration and Guided Practice Stage* and *Independent Production Stage*.

During the *Demonstration and Guided Practice Stage*, the teacher might informally construct **ThinkLinks** on charts, boards, a projector, or computer for several weeks before introducing a **ThinkLink kind**. This stage includes more structure, direction, modeling, and interaction than in the *Independent Production Stage*. The teacher uses prepared **ThinkLink** skeletal formats to a greater extent with primary students in order to encourage an in-depth understanding of the **ThinkLink** strategy.

For both primary and intermediate students, the *Independent Production Stage* is the stage at which a **ThinkLink kind** is integrated into the routine of the classroom. This third stage is at a high point when students decide what thinking **type**, what **kind** of **ThinkLink** (starting point), and what shape, or **form**, to select. When this final stage is reached for all four basic **kinds**, and when students know how to use the **ThinkLinks** as discussion formats and as **blueprints** for written composition, the response-to-reading program is in place in the classroom.

The chapter on Character **ThinkLinks** is written in more detail to give a clearer picture of an instructional procedure and is meant to suggest a way to teach the other three kinds. Teachers reading the book are encouraged to extrapolate to their own level if the samples and procedures seem to be more appropriate for younger or older students.

The book is intended for grades 1–8, though a kindergarten, secondary, or college teacher can adapt the ideas and procedures in any content area. The ordering of the four chapters is a suggested sequence for introducing and understanding **ThinkLinks**, though it is not necessary to teach a complete chapter before going on to the next. Within the chapters, suggestions are made for the sequencing of instruction, but other than the importance of teacher modeling, guided practice, and the ordering from simple to more complex, the teacher can decide when and how to introduce each activity.

There is a large body of literature and field-testing on variations related to **ThinkLinks**, though the **ThinkLink Classroom** suggested in this book is unique in its metacognitive and instructional dimensions. Some of the numerous labels for these variations are: cognitive mapping, webbing, semantic webbing, mind mapping, graphic organizers, and visual organizers. **ThinkLinks** has been found to be the most student-friendly term. The current interests in critical and creative thinking, the writing process, reading assessments, reading comprehension, the reading-writing connection, differentiated learning, multiple intelligences, learning strategies, cultural diversity, brain research, the engaged classroom, and emotional intelligence are well served by teacher and student expertise in the shaping and understanding of thought.

THE THINKLINK CLASSROOM

The ThinkLink metacognitive mapping strategy fits any framework in which the generation and organization of knowledge is crucial. Although there are no absolute ingredients to a program incorporating ThinkLinks, there are key instructional elements that accompany the strategy. Some of these are mentioned in the Introduction but, for clarity, are further described as part of the ThinkLink Classroom. The main categories for these elements are cueing, **Wait Time**, cooperative learning, written composition, assessment, and metacognitive question and response with the ThinkTrix. In this classroom, students are motivated to reach their fullest potential as readers, writers, and thinkers.

Cueing

In order to effectively utilize ThinkLinks, students and teachers need to see prototypical shapes as well as the student work samples that illustrate previous accomplishments. The work samples of ThinkLinks are cued on the wall or placed accessibly. Each of the four kinds of ThinkLinks—Character, Event, Theme, and Story—are displayed in different shapes, or forms, and in the various types of thinking, which are **Recall, Cause/Effect, Similarity** (analogy), **Difference, Idea→Example, Example→Idea,** and sometimes **Evaluation**. These are individual, group, or whole class products. In addition, all conceivable prototypical shapes, or forms, such as the web, wheel, and dangling boxes, are displayed as cueing devices and added to as they are invented, as shown on pages xiii through xiv.

When using ThinkLinks with reading and literature, the teacher and students generate and list for reference: characters, themes, stories, character traits/feelings, concepts, and major events. These class lists can be wall cued. Students may make and keep individual lists for working independently. The thinking matrix, or ThinkTrix, is charted, or at least the thinking types and sometimes sample questions are wall cued. Students may have copies of the ThinkTrix and other manipulative tools containing the seven thinking types, as shown on pages 2, 6, and 7, and in the Appendix on pages 83 through 85.

The use of prototypical shapes, or forms, work samples, lists, and teacher/student tools renders the ThinkLink metacognitive strategy more systematic and fluent. Under the pressure of classroom dynamics, students and teachers should not have to depend exclusively upon memory to know how to inquire, what and how to connect.

Wait Time

All group sharing or cooperative learning should be preceded by independent thought. Whether the thinking time, or Wait Time, is three seconds or even longer, as with writing or constructing ThinkLinks, independent thought is crucial. The classroom simply doesn't function as an inclusive learning culture unless all students have a chance to think. The question, or prompt, is the cue to begin thinking.

The secret to Wait Time is the teacher's (or student's) cueing of when students are to end thinking and raise hands or share with a partner. There is also **Wait Time II**, which is the interval between student responses. In this interval, students can consider the shared response and think on their own. This can be achieved during class discussion by the teacher's cueing for hands to be raised after a student speaks. In addition, Wait Time II can be structured according to thinking type. For example, the teacher can ask or cue students to respond to other students by thinking of examples of the shared idea, an analogy to an example, or cause and effect. The ensuing conversation may or may not include the teacher's comments.

The effects of time to think can easily be noted by increased participation, greater elaboration, more focus on the speaker, responses closely related to the question, better retention, improved behavior, more variation in teacher questioning, and generally more engaged class discussion.

Cooperative Learning

Students working in pairs and small groups can effectively generate and organize thought on ThinkLinks and use them as discussion maps or written composition blueprints. The ThinkLinks act as a focusing structure for cooperative learning. When students are experienced with the procedures, they can respond to discussion questions, their own or the teacher's, by creating ThinkLinks.

A teaching technique that is especially important for the generation and organization of thought is one known as **Think-Pair-Share**. This discussion cycle technique allows for Think, or Wait Time, after every question, sometimes followed by discussion in pairs, and usually ends with some sharing in the total group. The key to this technique is the teacher's cueing of each mode or phase. Verbal cues, sound cues, or visual cues such as hand signals move students from one phase to the next. For instance, students cannot raise their hands after Think, or Wait Time, until a signal is given to pair or share. During the Think and Pair mode, the teacher has the option of asking the students to respond in writing, or by using ThinkLinks.

The pair discussion can be structured in multiple ways, allowing, for instance, for partners to take turns talking, to reach consensus, and to make or add ideas onto a ThinkLink. In a larger group discussion that follows, students can share their own or their partner's ideas, display their ThinkLinks, ask the group questions, and/or dramatize their responses.

Among other cooperative learning structures, such as some of those promoted by Spencer Kagan, the ThinkLink metacognitive strategy lends itself to Jigsaw. Individual *experts* create ThinkLinks from their information, share in *expert* groups, add to the ThinkLinks, and share their knowledge in *home* groups.

Written Composition

It is always possible to use a ThinkLink as an organizer, or blueprint, for written composition. Every ThinkLink is an outline of a sort, though some shapes are more conducive to crafting a piece of writing. Students write essays, written reports, literary analysis, comprehension responses, stories, and even notes from ThinkLinks. If a formal outline is required, the outline is also constructed from the ThinkLink. Aside from the use as a brainstorming or vocabulary-developing web, descriptive writing and poetry are generally not enhanced by the ThinkLink prewriting stage, since they are largely dependent upon intuition and require a considerable amount of visualizing and usually a less structured format.

Assessment

For teachers and students to evaluate learning, tangible products are necessary. The ThinkLink metacognitive mapping strategy gives student achievement a visibility not always as easily achieved through other media. The connection of part to whole, of Cause/Effect, of Idea→Example, and of Similarities demonstrates the anatomy and architecture of knowledge gained. Student, teacher, and parent can use the ThinkLinks as indicators of achievement in reading comprehension and not simply as recall.

When the ThinkLinks are used as blueprints for written composition, the structure and content of the composition can easily be evaluated. It can also be demonstrated by action research that metacognitive mapping improves the quality of expository writing.

The metacognitive awareness facilitated by the question—response thinking type cues of the ThinkTrix is crucial to the student's understanding of test prompts. A student who can say, "This is a Cause/Effect question" has a better chance of answering the question. Knowing how one is to think and how to shape the thought in a ThinkLink is certain to improve written response. Students' problems with reading comprehension are often caused by not understanding the question and not knowing how to organize the answer. The question to be displayed for students is, "How does my mind work to answer this question or solve this problem, and how could I shape my thought?"

Metacognitive Question and Response

In the classroom, all questions fit one thinking type or combination of types. Students become metacognitive when they know these thinking types, thereby becoming aware of how they think. Teachers and students can use the ThinkTrix to generate and respond to questions from their reading and other contexts. The examples below demonstrate the utility of the ThinkTrix.

Some examples of questions and their categories, as indicated on the following matrix, would be:

- What are the most important personality traits of Dorothy? (1f)
- What ideas, or themes, are in the parade scene in *The Emperor's New Clothes*? (2f)
- What are some examples of loss in *Johnny Tremain*? (3e)
- What is the most important theme in *The Wonderful Wizard of Oz*? Why do you think so? (4f, 4e)
- What are the main causes of the solution to Pinocchio's problem? (1b, 3b)
- Why do people fake? (3b. 3c)
- How is Crow Boy like Wilbur? (1c, 1f)

- Is the problem in *Charlotte's Web* like the one in *Bridge to Terabithia*? In what way? (3c, or 4c)
- How is the relationship between Charlotte and Wilbur different from that between Leslie and Jess? (1d, 1f, 3d)

The teacher introduces the thinking symbols, or icons, gradually, at first using them as cues to ask questions. The teacher then develops the concept of each thinking type by giving examples and allowing practice with creating questions and labeling them by type. At some point, most primary and intermediate students are ready to use the symbols, or icons, to create questions or give responses.

The teacher then introduces the focal points (character, event, theme/concept, story, and others) and shows students how to use the ThinkTrix to classify and create questions. Interwoven with this metacognitive activity, the students learn how to construct ThinkLinks that accommodate the answers, thereby shaping their thought.

Teacher and students can use an enlarged One-Sided ThinkTrix with coded grid cells as a wall cue for the **metacognitive typing** of thought and for the generation of questions and responses. Students can use the Two-Sided ThinkTrix Discussion Board as a desk tool for discourse between and among themselves. Both are found below on pages 6 and 7. The focal, or departure points, can be changed to fit content areas other than literature/reading. There are other **metacognitive** tools such as wheels and pinch card strips displaying the thinking types as found in the Appendix on pages 83 and 84. Students use these tools individually, in pairs, and in groups to type thinking and to create and respond to questions. Cubes, flash cards, and wall cards are some other metacognitive tools. The creation of questions and the recognition of the basic thinking types are means toward meaningful response, not ends in themselves.

ThinkTrix: One-Sided

One-sided ThinkTrix can be used as a wall chart with groups or the entire class. When used as a guide for question creation or question type identification, it is helpful to have the grid cells coded as 1a, 1b, 2f, and so forth. Such matrices can be made for every content area by changing the focal or departure points.

	Character 1	Event 2	Feeling/Trait/ Theme 3	Story 4	Setting 5	Problem/ Conflict 6	Author's Style 7	Relationships 8
R Recall a	1a	2a	3a	4a	5a	6a	7a	8a
Cause ↔ Effect b	1b	2b	3b	4b	5b	6b	7b	8b
Similarity c	1c	2c	3c	4c	5c	6c	7c	8c
Difference d	1d	2d	3d	4d	5d	6d	7d	8d
Idea → Example(s) e	1e	2e	3e	4e	5e	6e	7e	8e
Example(s) → Idea(s) f	1f	2f	3f	4f	5f	6f	7f	8f
Evaluation g	1g	2g	3g	4g	5g	6g	7g	8g

ThinkTrix Discussion Board: Two-Sided Matrix

Students, individually or in pairs, sit on opposite sides of the board. Students on one side ask a question and place a marker on the cell(s) to indicate what type(s) of question(s) they are asking or answering. Students on the other side confirm or doubt the classification and try to respond. A high quality conversation, an in-depth understanding, and a deeper discussion are the main goals of this activity, along with the metacognitive aspect.

THINK TRIX Language Arts	R Recall	Cause and Effect	Similarities	Differences	Idea to Example(s)	Example(s) to Idea(s)	Evaluation	THINK TRIX Language Arts
Character								Character
Event								Event
Feeling/Trait/ Theme								Feeling/Trait/ Theme
Story								Story
Setting								Setting
Problem/ Conflict								Problem/ Conflict
Author's Style								Author's Style
Relationship								Relationship
THINK TRIX *Language Arts*	**R** Recall	Cause and Effect	Similarities	Differences	Idea to Example(s)	Example(s) to Idea(s)	Evaluation	**THINK TRIX** *Language Arts*

Belinda Miller/Frank Lyman/Sam Pollack/Shirley Rogers/Carla Beachy 1984-1990

Types of Thinking: ThinkTrix Question Examples and Starters

The highest level of metacognition is reached when students create questions with reference only to the thinking types on the icons, with or without the ThinkTrix matrix. However, question examples or starters can be used until students and teacher are able to craft questions without them.

RECALL

➡ What does _____ do?

➡ Who is _____ ?

➡ When does/do _____ come home?

➡ Where does/do _____ live?

Types of Thinking: ThinkTrix Question Examples and Starters (*Continued*)

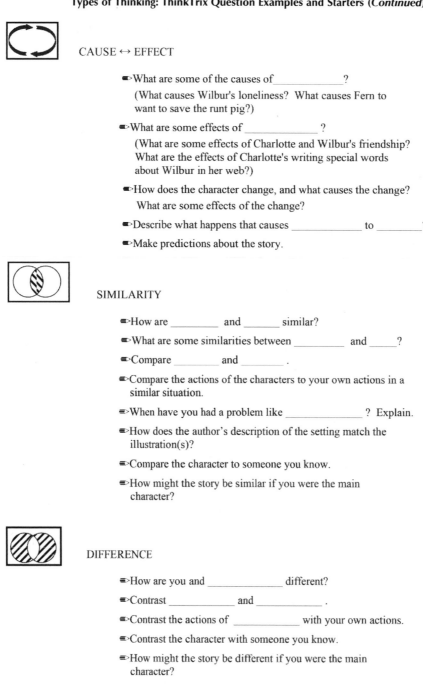

CAUSE ↔ EFFECT

☞What are some of the causes of _____ ?
(What causes Wilbur's loneliness? What causes Fern to want to save the runt pig?)

☞What are some effects of _____ ?
(What are some effects of Charlotte and Wilbur's friendship? What are the effects of Charlotte's writing special words about Wilbur in her web?)

☞How does the character change, and what causes the change? What are some effects of the change?

☞Describe what happens that causes _____ to _____ ?

☞Make predictions about the story.

SIMILARITY

☞How are _____ and _____ similar?

☞What are some similarities between _____ and ____?

☞Compare _____ and _____ .

☞Compare the actions of the characters to your own actions in a similar situation.

☞When have you had a problem like _____ ? Explain.

☞How does the author's description of the setting match the illustration(s)?

☞Compare the character to someone you know.

☞How might the story be similar if you were the main character?

DIFFERENCE

☞How are you and _____ different?

☞Contrast _____ and _____ .

☞Contrast the actions of _____ with your own actions.

☞Contrast the character with someone you know.

☞How might the story be different if you were the main character?

IDEA → EXAMPLE(S)

☞What are some examples of_____ ? (What are some examples of Broderick's determination?)

☞What are some examples of the (theme) in the story?

Types of Thinking: ThinkTrix Question Examples and Starters (*Continued*)

➡️ What are some stories that have (name of theme) as a theme? (What are some stories that have "friendship" as a theme?)

➡️ What are some examples of realistic or fantasy events in the story?

➡️ What are some examples of stories that are fiction? (What are some examples of stories that are adventure fiction?)

➡️ What are some examples of sensory imagery in the story?

➡️ What are some examples of figurative language in the story?

EXAMPLE(S) → IDEA(S)

➡️ What kind of person is _____?

➡️ What are some traits that describe _____?

➡️ What are some feelings that _____ had?

➡️ What is a main problem or conflict in this selection?

➡️ What are some problems that _____ faces?

➡️ Summarize the selection in one to three sentences.

➡️ What are some of the important ideas in the selection?

➡️ What are some themes in the story/novel?

➡️ What is the story's message?

➡️ What is the moral or lesson of the story?

➡️ Using context clues, tell what the word _____ means?

➡️ When _____ said "_____", what did he/she mean?

➡️ _____, _____, and _____ are all examples of _____?

EVALUATION

➡️ Do you like/dislike the story? Tell why.

➡️ What parts of the story do you like the best? Explain.

➡️ If you could change one part of the story, what would you change? Explain.

➡️ Is it right (wrong) for _____ to _____? Explain.

➡️ Is it fair (unfair) for to _____? Explain.

➡️ Does _____ make the right choice to _____? Explain.

➡️ Do you think it is good, bad, right, or wrong for _____?

➡️ What do you think _____ could have done to solve/avoid the problem/situation?

➡️ Do you agree with _____? Why?

➡️ Should have done _____? Why or why not?

➡️ What advice would you give to _____ about _____?

➡️ Do you think the title is a good one for the chapter, story, or novel?

A THINKLINK PRIMARY CLASSROOM SCENARIO

In both the primary and intermediate scenarios that follow, the focus of these classrooms is the generation and connection of student ideas and examples. Instructional activities are designed to engage students' critical and independent thinking and questioning. These interactive learning environments encourage students to support and assist one another, to work cooperatively, and to praise and celebrate one another's efforts and accomplishments. At the same time, an enthusiasm for learning is instilled, confidence and self-worth are fostered, and emphasizing strengths and talents is supported.

When entering the primary language arts classroom in late fall, one is enveloped by a variety of ThinkLinks and large charts of students' ideas created since the first weeks of school. In one corner is a large yarn web with a dangling spider hanging from the ceiling that publicizes ThinkLinks. Displayed on the walls are **ThinkLink** prototype shapes such as wheels, webs, and analogy links; the ThinkTrix icons for **Recall, Cause-Effect, Similarity, Difference, Idea-Example, Example-Idea,** and **Evaluation**; and large charts of traits/feelings and themes developed by the teacher and students.

Also part of the classroom environment are many student products such as trait/feeling **Concept Webs** and personal trait/feeling **Me Webs** with sentence examples and artistic embellishments. Colorful charts with webs of characters such as Broderick and Crow Boy illustrate their traits/feelings with supporting examples. Shared in literature class discussions, they are then displayed on the walls or hang from the ceiling.

In the front of the room, the teacher is working with one reading group sitting in a circle. Students have their books, their **Character Webs** completed the previous day, and their individual **literature journals** with them. On the board is a large chart of colored paper. The teacher asks guiding and probing questions that encourage students to share traits/ feelings of the main character and supporting example events from their webs. Students support their ideas by revisiting their texts to read aloud selections that support and clarify their responses.

During this discussion, the teacher uses Wait Time and often has students **Think-Pair-Share** ideas before responding with the entire literature circle. They often make corrections, changes, and additions to their own webs. Any new traits/ feelings shared during the discussion are added to the composite chart and to their personal lists in their literature journals. The teacher encourages students to share the most significant traits/feelings as well as events so that the composite charted **Character Web** shows the major problem, the solution, and the choices involving the character, but also character change and development. This composite **Character Web** of student ideas, a magnum opus of the group responses and interactions, is then displayed in the classroom.

Meanwhile, another reading group has students paired with study partners working quietly at their desks or in a designated area of the classroom. They are taking turns re-reading an assigned story and asking each other questions that were previously written on their **Question Generator**, as found in the Appendix on page 85. The *Types of Thinking ThinkTrix Question Examples and Starters* found on pages 8 and 9 further assisted them. Later, during the Language Arts period or on the next day, the teacher has a circle discussion in which students share their questions, use pinch cards to **type** questions asked, and respond to the questions. The teacher may choose to chart the most insightful and fruitful questions that then become models for further questions.

Students in a third reading group working independently at their desks, having read a story, and having had a circle discussion with the teacher that resulted in a charted **Character Web**, are now completing Character Comparison ThinkLinks to show similarities between themselves and the significant character previously discussed. The following day, the teacher may choose to have students share their Character Comparison ThinkLinks and perhaps even use their ThinkLinks as blueprints for writing short paragraphs.

ThinkLink activities progress on the following days. Some students working in pairs or fours are beginning to use parts of the **ThinkTrix Discussion Board** during language arts. The teacher listens in on the conversations. During the sharing of novels in literature class discussions, the teacher continues to construct webs of significant characters, thus expanding students' knowledge of traits/feelings, the importance of choices made by characters, and how characters have changed or developed. Students often share Similarities and Differences between and among characters and themselves. The teacher continues to add student ideas from literature class discussions and reading groups to a **Big Idea Theme Web on Friendship** showing multiple examples of friendship in fiction and in their lives. In addition, webs, wheels, and other ThinkLinks showing student ideas in math, social studies, and science are displayed on the walls.

The Primary ThinkLink Classroom offers a learning environment that embraces structure as well as flexibility and that encompasses critical thinking activities that are creative and challenging, yet not frustrating. Most important, the focus of the primary classroom is the generation and connection of students' ideas and examples. The following is an example of a **ThinkTrix Question Generator** for primary students.

ThinkTrix Question Generator: Primary

Topic: __The_Little_Red_Hen____

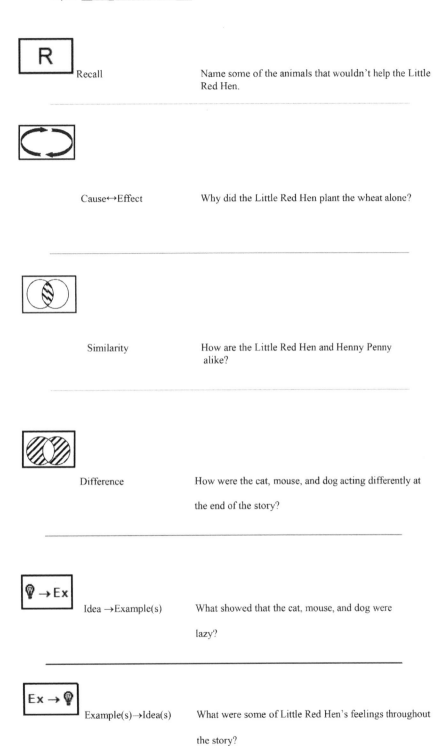

Recall   Name some of the animals that wouldn't help the Little
                                      Red Hen.

Cause↔Effect   Why did the Little Red Hen plant the wheat alone?

Similarity   How are the Little Red Hen and Henny Penny
                                      alike?

Difference   How were the cat, mouse, and dog acting differently at

                                      the end of the story?

Idea →Example(s)   What showed that the cat, mouse, and dog were

                                      lazy?

Example(s)→Idea(s)   What were some of Little Red Hen's feelings throughout

                                      the story?

Evaluation   Should the Little Red Hen have eaten the cake all

                                      by herself?   Why or why not?

A THINKLINK INTERMEDIATE CLASSROOM SCENARIO

When entering **The Intermediate ThinkLink Classroom**, the impression is one of purposeful activity. The teacher is charting student responses on a large web. The question at hand is "What traits and feelings from the story describe the development of the story's hero/heroine and how do the events support these traits and feelings?" Each student has had the opportunity to think, construct an individual web, and share with a partner before sharing with the teacher. When each student shares for the class composite web, other students listen carefully with hands down. The teacher accepts all relevant answers but motivates the students to find the most significant traits and feelings as well as supporting events.

After the composite class ThinkLink is sufficiently representative of the group's thinking, the students then return to an independent activity to further enrich their in-depth understanding of the story previously discussed. They are instructed to create their own question about the story, avoiding **Recall** questions. The students choose a type of thinking from the cued ThinkTrix thinking type icons or the large ThinkTrix wall chart and decide on a departure point such as Character, Event, or Idea/Theme. They then craft a question such as "What effects did the character's choice have on his/her friends? How is the character like a character in *The Wonderful Wizard of Oz*? What is a main theme of the story, and what events demonstrate its importance? What causes the prejudice in the story, and what are the causes of prejudice in general? How is the plot of the story different from that of *Charlotte's Web*? Is it right for the hero/heroine to make that decision? Why or why not? In this scene, what are the important feelings and ideas?"

When students have their questions and have labeled them as to type, they look at the many wall-cued ThinkLink shapes, or forms, and choose the most appropriate prototype shape for the question. They then select or create ThinkLink shapes to the answer to their own question.

Following this independent activity, the teacher brings the students into a circle to share their questions and ThinkLinks. Students can identify verbally, with pinch cards found in the Appendix on page 83 or using hand signals, the type or types of thinking required to answer the question. They then share responses and ThinkLinks that justify their thinking.

On some days at the point when the students have created a question, they ask it of a partner and a pair conversation follows, each student adding to a ThinkLink, or, in some cases, simply discussing. This discussion can take place over a matrix where each student in the pair can see types of thinking and focal or departure points. When using the two-sided matrix, or **ThinkTrix Discussion Board** found on page 7, the students in pairs or fours can generate more questions, discuss, and sometimes ThinkLink many aspects of the story and related stories. The students can also use the enlarged ThinkTrix wall cue in which the matrix cells are identified.

As the students work individually or in groups, the teacher interacts, listening and helping. The emphasis is upon the quality of the thinking. Are students probing the character's choices, motives, causes, effects, and/or changes? Are they relating the story to life experience and other stories through themes, ideas, characters, and events? Do they see the effects of ethical decisions? Once again, the teacher may choose to have a circle discussion where questions and responses are shared.

On subsequent days, the teacher may ask students to write responses or essays based on their ThinkLinks. These responses or essays not only are profound in themselves but also can be used as models for further writing. In addition, students can be asked to re-create in writing or improvisational drama the events or scenes from the story that are most significant for their answers. When the teacher reads aloud dramatically the re-created scenes, or the students perform the improvisations in small groups, the class has reached another level in understanding literature.

Of the many choices open to the class, at this point, one option is to take a universal theme of the book such as friendship, prejudice, or conflict and search for examples from literature. Once students have formed enough examples of the theme using a wall-cued story list and/or their personal lists, the teacher can construct with them a class composite ThinkLink displaying the connections to the theme. The inquiry can then proceed to questions such as "What causes friendship? What are its effects? How are these conflicts alike and different? How can prejudice be prevented?" As they discuss, construct ThinkLinks, and sometimes write essays on these questions, as shown on pages 89 through 96, they are building foundational structures of knowledge.

There are many other possible scenarios to the Intermediate ThinkLink Classroom. Teachers who understand the essence of the strategy will create their own.

ThinkTrix Question Generator: Intermediate/Secondary

Students respond well to the structure of the Question Generator. They write a question in every box. Using this tool, they can ask and answer their own comprehension questions or classify questions from the text or test.

Topic: _____

R **Recall**

_____

Cause↔Effect

Similarity

Difference

Idea →Example(s)

Example(s)→Idea(s)

Evaluation

Chapter 1

The Character ThinkLink

The Character **ThinkLink** focuses on major or minor characteristics, exploits, and development of characters in stories. There are two **varieties** of Character ThinkLinks: the individual Character Web, which focuses on one character, and the Character Comparison ThinkLink, which compares two or more characters.

PART I: THE CHARACTER WEB

Definition, Prototypes, and Samples

The Character Web is a ThinkLink that identifies traits or feelings exhibited by a character as well as happenings from the character's life that exemplify these traits/feelings. These examples could be events, relationships, problems, or choices. In constructing a Character Web, one proceeds from an example(s) to a related character trait/feeling and/or from a trait/feeling to a related example(s). In other words, the web is constructed from the concrete to the abstract (Example→Idea) and/or the reverse (Idea→Example). In placing the thinking on the Character Web, the teacher or student writes an example—often an event—and derives one or more traits or feelings or begins with a trait or feeling and attaches one or more supporting examples, or both, as shown in Figures 1.1 to 1.3.

One purpose of the Character Web is to help the student gain insight into a character. After webbing, the student better understands key events in a character's life and how these events influence and shape the character. As the character develops, the student can more readily understand this development.

There are at least three separate emphases involved in character analysis. The simplest **variety** of Character Web is one in which traits or feelings are derived events in random order and without attention to importance, basically a brainstorming activity. Another variety that sometimes follows the first is a randomly organized web in which only important traits or feelings are emphasized. Finally, there are chronologically ordered webs in which the development of the character is the focus. With this latter variety, students learn how the key events, relationships, problems, solutions, or choices in the story influence and shape the character.

Figures 1.1 to 1.3 are prototypes that show the linking of character traits/feelings and examples. Examine them carefully before reading about the instructional process. The thinking **type** classifications in brackets throughout the book are below the figure numbers. These classifications are from the **Modified ThinkTrix** on page 2 and the complete **One-Sided ThinkTrix** on page 6.

**Character Web
Figure 1.1
[1f]**

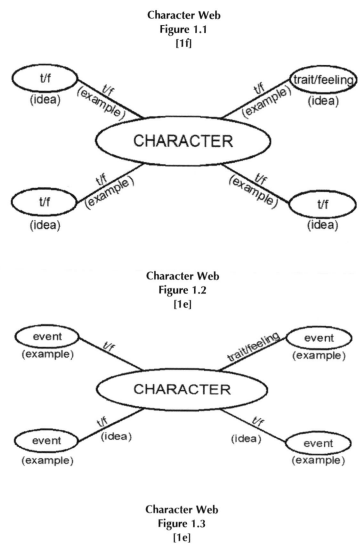

**Character Web
Figure 1.2
[1e]**

**Character Web
Figure 1.3
[1e]**

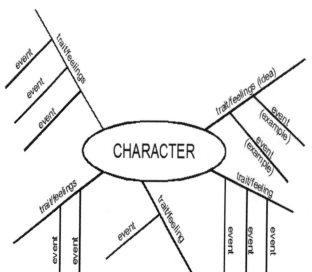

The following samples show the linking of character traits/feelings and examples, as shown in Figures 1.4 through 1.6. The samples shown are produced at all stages of the ThinkLink process.

Character Web
Figure 1.4
[1e]

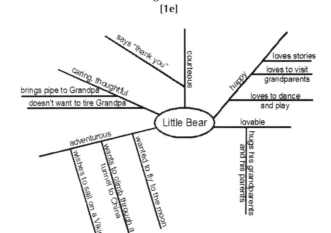

Character Web
Figure 1.5
[1e]

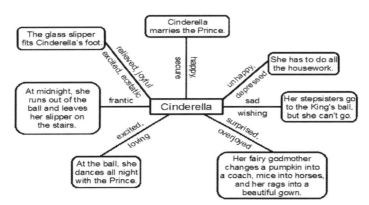

Character Web
Figure 1.6
[1f]

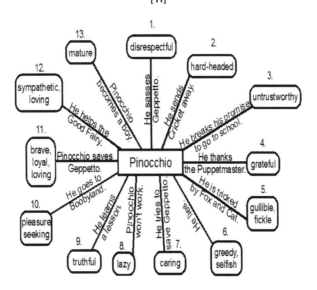

Instruction

During the initial ThinkLink instruction, it is especially important for students to progress at a pace that is challenging, yet not frustrating. Since there are numerous possibilities for Character Webs at varying degrees of difficulty, the instruction for these webs proceeds from the simple to the complex. The student gains confidence at each level of difficulty. Consideration is given to the student's developmental and reading level. Students work individually and/or in pairs, and at later stages experiment with and invent different ThinkLink shapes, artistic designs, and color-coding.

The instruction for the Character Web, as with other ThinkLink instruction, includes two basic stages: *Demonstration and Guided Practice Stage* and the *Independent Production Stage.*

During the *Demonstration and Guided Practice Stage*, the teacher models by constructing a large Character Web on the basis of a fairy tale, folk tale, short story, or another context involving a familiar literary character. After presenting the story, the teacher diagrams the students' responses to questions regarding the main character's traits or feelings and the related examples in the story.

For the web construction, the teacher uses two basic questioning/reasoning approaches: concrete to abstract (Example→Idea) or abstract to concrete (Idea→Example). The two approaches are intermingled as the teacher helps students derive the trait/feelings of a story character from events involving the character (Example→Idea) and then connect other events to the derived traits/feelings (Idea→Example). The ThinkLink can be centered on the traits/feelings with connecting events as in Figures 1.4 and 1.5 or on the events with connecting traits/feelings as in Figure 1.6.

Following are some questions illustrative of those leading to the construction of the Character Web. The questions are labeled according to the type of the thinking required in which to answer. The questions elicit either random traits/feelings or character development.

- What is something that happens to _____? [R]
- How does this make _____ feel? [Example→Idea]
- What is an important event that happens to_____, and how does _____ feel? [R, Example→Idea]
- What are some character traits of_____? [Example→Idea]
- What does _____ do that that shows this trait? [Idea→Example]
- What are some feelings that_____ has and what events show these feelings? [Example→Idea; Idea→Example]
- What problem does _____ experience? [Example→Idea]
- How is the problem finally solved? [Idea→Example]
- What does the solution show about_____' character? [Example→Idea]
- What are important choices made by___? [Idea→Example]
- What do these choices say about___? [Example→Idea]
- What kind of person is ___ at the beginning? [Example→Idea]
- In what ways does_____ change? [Idea→Example; Example→Idea]
- Give some examples of how _____ changes. [Idea→Example]
- What traits does _____ show at the end? [Example→Idea]
- At the end what does_____ do that shows change? [Idea→Example]

The teacher demonstrates both questioning/reasoning approaches and explains them on the ThinkTrix. The decision about which to use depends upon the nature of the character being analyzed, the teacher's style, and the students' developmental levels and knowledge of the story. However, some webs are a combination of both approaches.

Figures 1.7 to 1.9 and 1.12 show random brainstorming of traits/feelings and related examples. This brainstorming can be structured to find the most important events and traits/feelings. The teacher can move then to webs that show character development and that reveal key traits and feelings of the changing character, as shown in Figures 1.10 and 1.11. In this latter variation, attention is given to a character's main problem in the story, to how the problem is solved, and to the possible resulting character development or change.

The analysis of character development depends upon the nature of the story. In stories such as *Winnie the Pooh*, the characters remain the same, whereas in *Pinocchio*, the protagonist is a developing character. In each case the completed web now serves as a product of the teacher-student interaction. It may be displayed in the classroom as a model for future student-produced webs.

Even with this approach, when the initial reasoning begins as Example→Idea, the emphasis is upon verifying, or supporting, the idea by finding events, relationships, problems, solutions, and choices.

Character-Trait-Event Web
Figure 1.7
[1e]

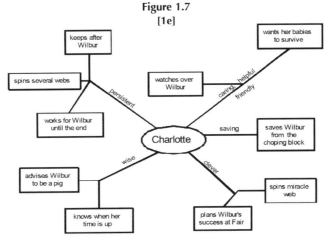

Character-Trait-Event Web
Figure 1.8
[1e]

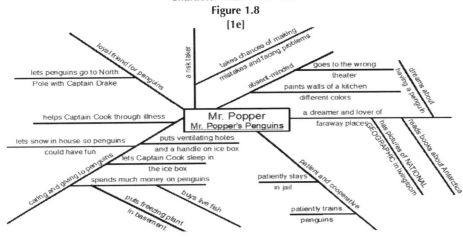

Character-Trait-Event Web
Figure 1.9
[1e]

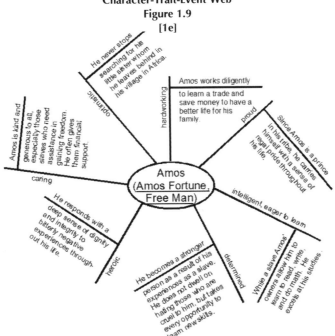

Character-Trait-Event Web
Figure 1.10
[1e]

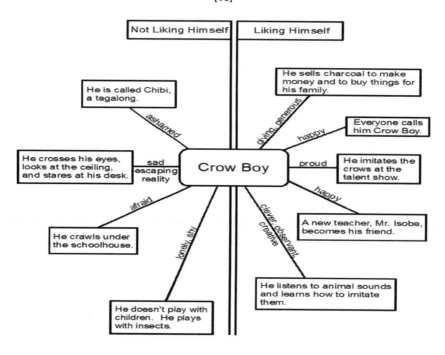

Character-Trait-Event Web
Figure 1.11
[1e]

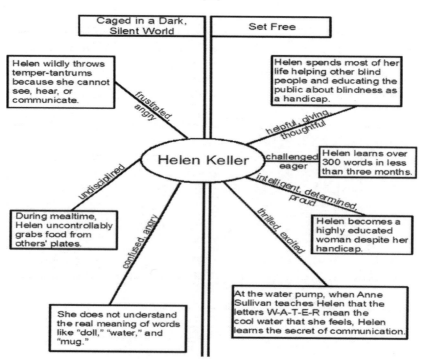

Character-Trait-Event Web
Figure 1.12
[1e]

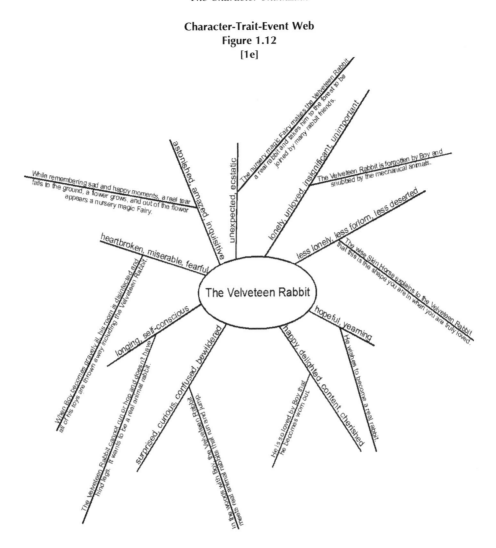

After student involvement in numerous teacher-directed Web constructions, the teacher often discovers that many students, especially at the intermediate level, have a thorough understanding of the ThinkLink metacognitive mapping strategy. The teacher continues to guide the students' progress by having them individually, or in pairs, create Character Webs and share their products during group discussion. The *Demonstration and Guided Practice Stage* is repeated each time the teacher introduces a new **kind, variety**, or **form** of ThinkLink.

However, during the *Demonstration and Guided Practice Stage* for the various kinds, varieties, and forms, the teacher may discover, especially at the primary level, that the students require more understanding of character traits and feelings. Should this be the case, the teacher spends time developing concepts by using **Trait or Feeling Webs** such as in Figures 1.13 through 1.15 and by using **Me Webs** such as those in Figure 1.16. In the latter web, the character is the student. Students are able to produce these personal explorations easily and see the similarity between literary character analysis and analysis of themselves.

Kind refers to focal, or departure point, such as Character, Event, Theme, and Story ThinkLinks. **Variety** refers to the kind of ThinkLink along with the type(s) of thinking involved. Form refers to a design, or a shape.

Concept Development Web
Figure 1.13
[3e]

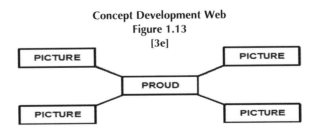

Concept Development Web
Figure 1.14
[3e]

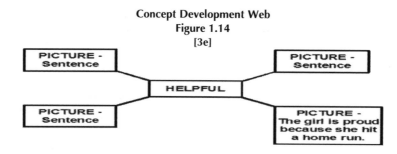

Concept Development Web
Figure 1.15
[1e]

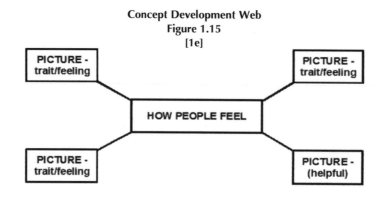

Character-Trait/Feeling Event Web
Figure 1.16
[1e]

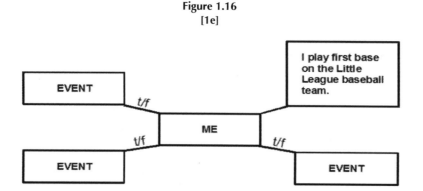

In conjunction with this guided concept development, the teacher begins to chart a list of character traits/feelings derived from a discussion of literature and the students' personal experiences. The concepts are developed with the students by using examples from literature and life and are randomly or categorically listed on a chart or in an individual booklet, or journal, for each student, as shown in the Appendix on pages 75 to 78. The list is displayed and serves as a cue during the *Demonstration and Guided Practice Stage* as well as sometimes during the *Independent Production Stage*. It is important to note that overdependence on the list may interfere with the students' deriving precise and relevant traits/feelings, since the true essence of the character's actions may not be on the list.

Once students gain confidence in their understanding of traits/feelings and confidence with the web shape, they will be ready to produce webs in response to a common frame of reference such as a story from the reading group or literature. During this guided practice, students construct Character Webs from reading selections. Especially for primary students, the teacher often uses partially completed **Skeletal Webs,** such as those shown in Figures 1.17 through 1.21 to lend structure. In this process, the teacher constructs a Skeletal Web worksheet or chart on the basis of a story giving a trait/feeling, page number, or event to lend support and guidance. The students then complete the Skeletal Webs by determining traits/feelings and/or related examples (problems/solutions, choices, conclusions, and relationships).

Skeletal Character Web
Figure 1.17
[1e]

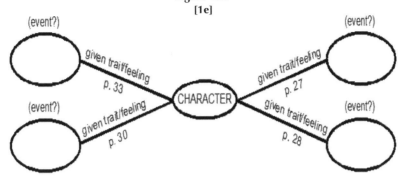

Skeletal Character Web
Figure 1.18
[1e]

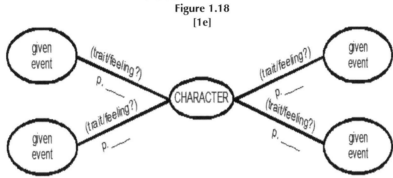

Skeletal Character Web
Figure 1.19
[1e]

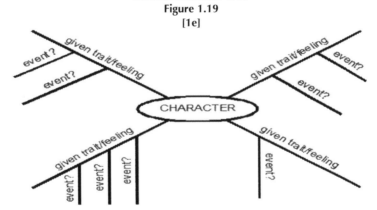

Skeletal Character Web
Figure 1.20
[1f]

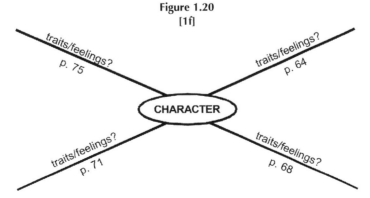

Skeletal Character Web
Figure 1.21
[1e]

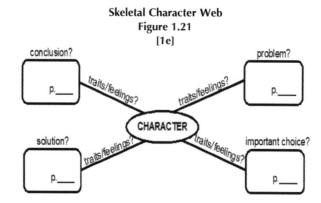

After the students complete skeletal Character Webs individually or in pairs, they often join in a teacher-group discussion to share ideas. The teacher charts a large composite Web that becomes the focus and guide for the discussion. The teacher tries to ensure that the students achieve an in-depth understanding of the character by encouraging them to make the most accurate connections between ideas and examples and by encouraging them to cite passages from the text. When the composite web includes only traits/feelings, the supporting examples are verbalized by the students rather than by the teacher. Students continue this process until they are adept at deriving traits/feelings (ideas) as in Figures 1.22 through 1.24 and traits/feelings (ideas) to examples as in Figures 1.25 through 1.27.

Character Web
Figure 1.22
[1f]

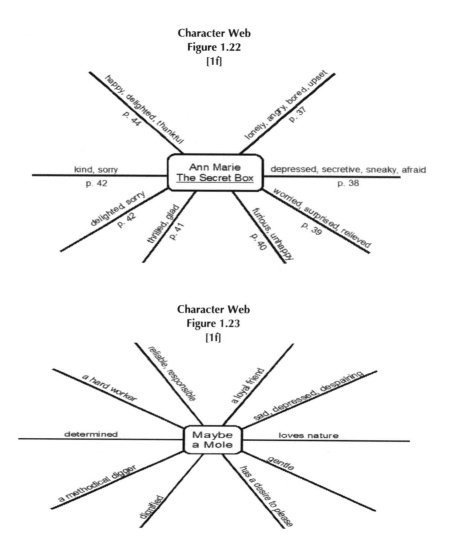

Character Web
Figure 1.23
[1f]

Character Web
Figure 1.24
[1f]

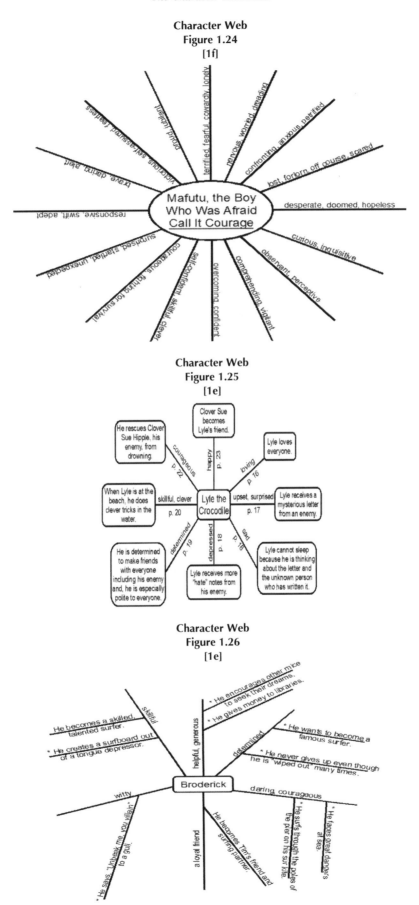

Character Web
Figure 1.25
[1e]

Character Web
Figure 1.26
[1e]

Character Web
Figure 1.27
[1e]

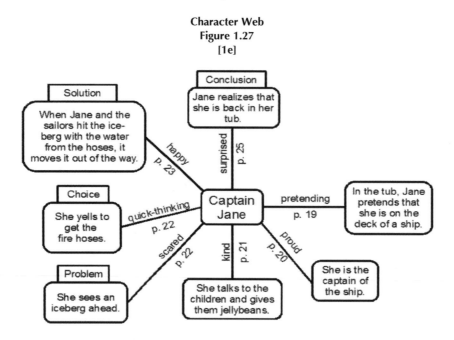

The ThinkLink process continues with all students constructing Character Webs individually, or in pairs, with as much teacher direction and support as necessary during *the Demonstration and Guided Practice Stage*. The teacher and students construct and display large Character Webs as follow-ups to reading stories, literature, films, selected television programs, or real-life experiences.

If there is character development, such as in *Pinocchio, Crow Boy,* and *Helen Keller,* it is important for the students to understand how and why the character changes. If there is little or no character development, as in *Winnie the Pooh,* the most central character traits/feelings and the related examples such as problem and solution become the center of analysis. It is important to note that the composite webbing and discussion is a learning experience in itself and not necessarily a blueprint for written composition. The final charted Character Web stands as an end product of the discussion and once again may be displayed in the classroom for future reference.

After students have had the guided practice, they begin the *Independent Production Stage* in which they make their ThinkLinks independently, selecting or deriving traits/feelings, and identifying key examples within the main plot of the story that support these traits/feelings. The generation of original insights is encouraged. Character analysis and the in-depth dimensions are thereby enhanced.

After the students complete skeletal Character Webs individually or in pairs, they often join in a teacher-group discussion to share ideas. Throughout the discussion and charting of a large composite Character Web, the teacher again tries to ensure that the Web functions as a tool for achieving in-depth understanding of the character. The composite Character Web becomes the focus and guide for the discussion.

The teacher facilitates the quality of student responses by giving **Think Time** and **Pair Talk** and encouraging students to listen carefully to the sharing of ideas and to cite passages to confirm, disprove, or clarify an example or trait/feeling. The teacher-constructed composite Web, the charting of ideas from the students' Character Webs, and the verbal interaction during the discussion is an integral part of the ThinkLink metacognitive strategy, as shown in Figures 1.28 and 1.31.

Throughout all discussions, the teacher refers to the types of thinking that students are using. The teacher encourages the students to identify how they are all thinking, using the ThinkTrix types.

The ultimate *Independent Production Stage* is one in which students have choices as to which **kind** and variety (by focal, or departure point, and thinking type), and form (variation of design, or shape) to generate and organize thought. They also select their own book(s) or story(s), create their own questions, use the **Two-Sided ThinkTrix Discussion Board**, run their own **Think-Pair-Share** discussions, write compositions, design the ThinkLinks cooperatively, and use color coding and art work to embellish the designs.

In this stage, students have a high degree of ownership of the learning process, and, whereas intermediate or advanced primary students more easily reach the stage, the goal is to render all students able to create personal meaning from literature. At this point, students are able to function well independently, as is evidenced by the originality of design and the complexity in their ThinkLinks.

Character-Trait-Event Web
Figure 1.28
[1e]

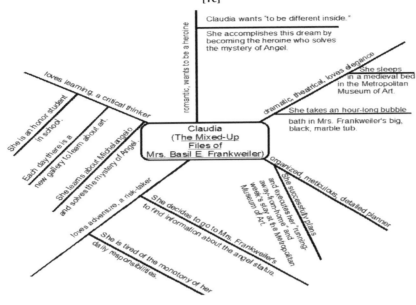

Change of Character
Figure 1.29
[1f]

Maybe A Mole

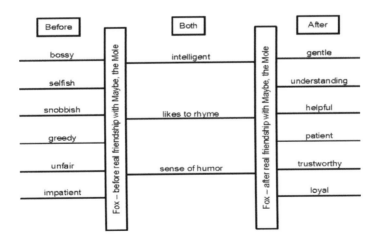

Character Web
Figure 1.30
[1f]

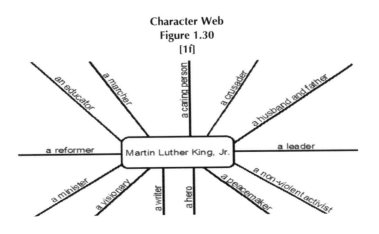

Character-Trait-Event Web
Figure 1.31
[1e]

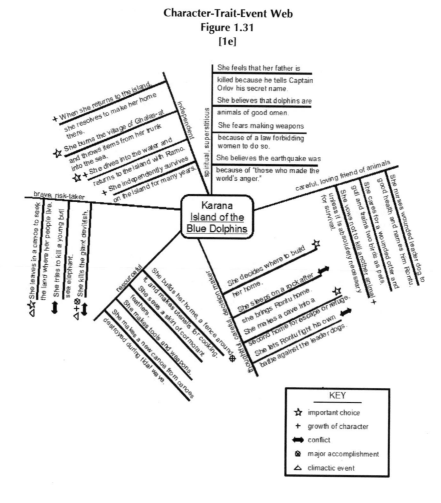

PART II: THE CHARACTER COMPARISON THINKLINK

Definitions and Prototypes

A Character Comparison ThinkLink variety compares two or more characters by linking their similarities and identifying differences. Characters are compared on the basis of circumstances, problems, solutions, choices, life events, relationships, traits, and feelings.

The following are prototypes of Character Comparison ThinkLinks, as shown in Figures 1.32 through 1.41.

Character-Trait/Feeling Comparison ThinkLink
Figure 1.32
[1c, 1f]

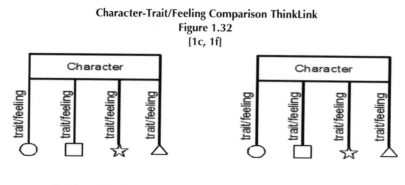

Character-Trait/Feeling Comparison ThinkLink
Figure 1.33
[1c, 1e]

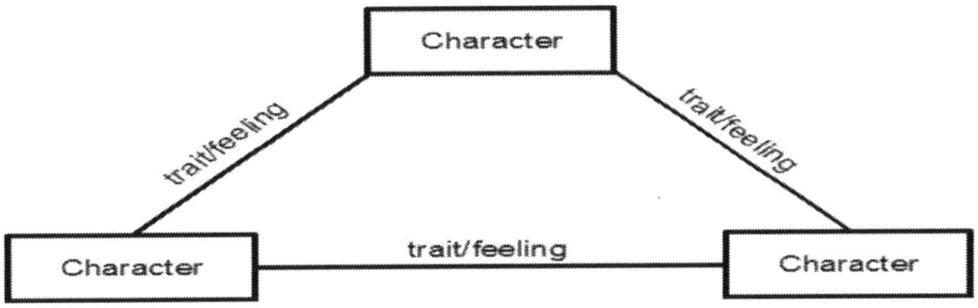

```
                    ┌──────────────┐
                    │  Character   │
                    └──────────────┘
         trait/feeling              trait/feeling
  ┌──────────────┐                      ┌──────────────┐
  │  Character   │───trait/feeling──────│  Character   │
  └──────────────┘                      └──────────────┘
```

Character-Trait/Feeling Comparison ThinkLink
Figure 1.34
[1c, 1e]

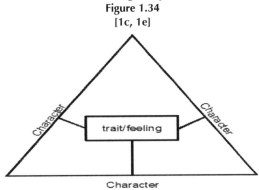

Character-Trait/Feeling Comparison ThinkLink
Figure 1.35
[1c, 1e, 1f]

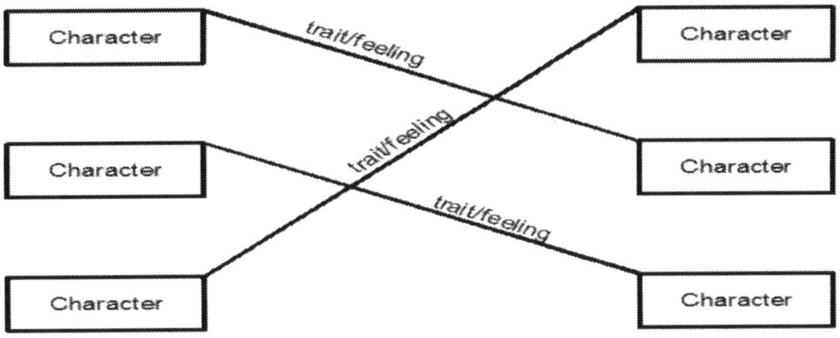

```
┌──────────────┐                          ┌──────────────┐
│  Character   │          trait/feeling   │  Character   │
└──────────────┘                          └──────────────┘

┌──────────────┐       trait/feeling      ┌──────────────┐
│  Character   │                          │  Character   │
└──────────────┘                          └──────────────┘

┌──────────────┐          trait/feeling   ┌──────────────┐
│  Character   │                          │  Character   │
└──────────────┘                          └──────────────┘
```

Character-Trait/Feeling Comparison ThinkLink
Figure 1.36
[1c, 1d, 1f]

<u>Differences</u>　　　<u>Similarities</u>　　　<u>Differences</u>

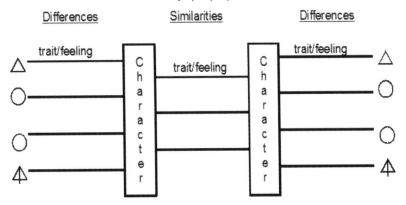

Character-Trait/Feeling Comparison ThinkLink
Figure 1.37
[1c, 1f]

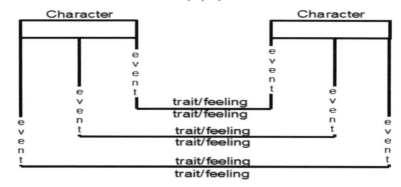

Trait/Feeling Event Comparison ThinkLink
Figure 1.38
[1c, 1e, 1f]

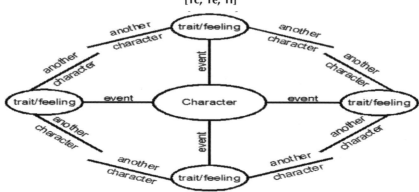

Character-Event Comparison ThinkLink
Figure 1.39
[1c, 2c]

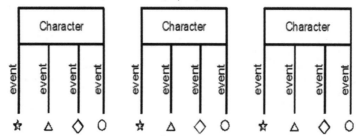

Character-Event Comparison ThinkLink
Figure 1.40
[1c, 1f, 2c]

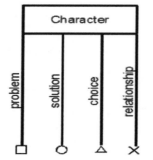
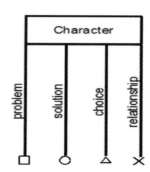

Character-Ratio Comparison ThinkLink
Figure 1.41
[1c, 1f]

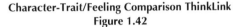

Instruction

In introducing the Character Comparison ThinkLink to students at any level, the teacher selects from the text or literature two similar characters familiar to the group. During the *Demonstration and Guided Practice Stage*, the teacher asks the students to consider either the similarity of traits/feelings or the similarity of events, circumstances, solutions, problems, choices, or relationships in the experiences of both characters. During the discussion, the teacher constructs a large Character Comparison ThinkLink of the students' responses.

Since analogy making is a complex process, the teacher may want to delay the introduction of this variety of Character ThinkLink until the basic Event, Theme, and Story ThinkLinks have been taught.

Students are encouraged to find examples to support their ideas. Also, especially with primary students, a comparison between the student and a literary character is illuminating and motivational. Figures 1.42 through 1.46 are samples of Character Comparison ThinkLinks.

Character-Trait/Feeling Comparison ThinkLink
Figure 1.42
[1c,1f]

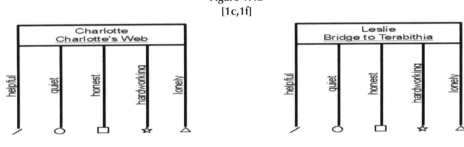

Character-Trait/Feeling Comparison ThinkLink
Figure 1.43
[1c, 1e, 1f]

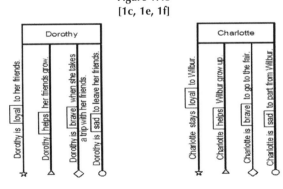

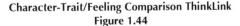

Character-Trait/Feeling Comparison ThinkLink
Figure 1.44
[1c, 1e, 1f]

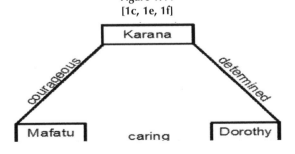

Character-Trait/Feeling Comparison ThinkLink
Figure 1.45
[1c, 1f]

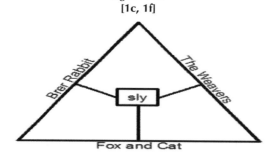

Character-Trait/Feeling Comparison ThinkLink
Figure 1.46
[1c, 1e, 1f]

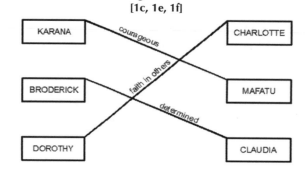

Character-Trait/Feeling Comparison ThinkLink
Figure 1.47
[1c, 1d, 1f]

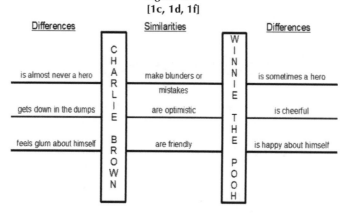

Character-Trait/Feeling Comparison ThinkLink
Figure 1.48
[1c, 1f]

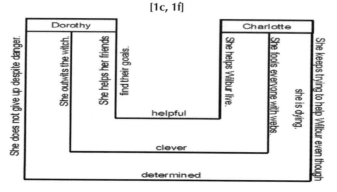

Character-Trait/Feeling Comparison ThinkLink
Figure 1.49
[1c, 1e, 1f]

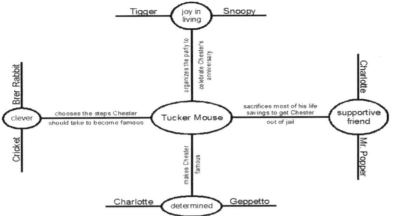

Character-Event Comparison ThinkLink
Figure 1.50
[1c, 2c]

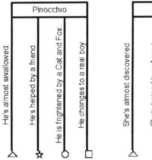

Character-Event/Idea Comparison ThinkLink
Figure 1.51
[1c, 1f, 2c]

Character-Ratio Analogy ThinkLink
Figure 1.52
[1c, 1f]

$$\frac{\text{Beauty}}{\text{Beast}} : \frac{\text{Boris}}{\text{Amos}} : \frac{\text{Charlotte}}{\text{Wilbur}} : \frac{\text{Karana}}{\text{Rontu}} : \frac{\text{Mary Poppins}}{\text{Trapp Children}} : \left(\text{help each other in important ways through love}\right)$$

$$\frac{\text{Tailors}}{\text{Emperor}} : \frac{\text{Fox and Cat}}{\text{Pinocchio}} : \frac{\text{Brom Bones}}{\text{Ichabod}} : \left(\text{take advantage of fear to trick}\right)$$

After each shape of Character Comparison ThinkLinks is demonstrated, the students construct ThinkLinks using characters from the text or literature. The teacher or the students select these characters. With teacher guidance and working independently or in pairs, students construct these ThinkLinks, as shown in part I of this chapter. As a follow-up, a group discussion is held in order to share the comparison. The teacher sometimes charts these ideas. During the discussion the teacher guides the students' thinking so that responses include the significant ways in which the characters are similar. If charted, this diagram functions as another model for future student-constructed Character Comparison ThinkLinks.

As with the instruction for all **ThinkLink kinds** and their **varieties**, the *Independent Production Stage* is one in which students work independently, choosing characters and selecting or inventing **ThinkLink** shapes, as shown on pages xiii through xiv. The Character Comparison **ThinkLinks** are ideal prewriting **blueprints** for written composition, as shown on pages 89 through 96.

SUMMARY

There are two varieties of Character ThinkLinks: Character Web and Character Comparison. The Character Web is probably the most advantageous way to begin the ThinkLink metacognitive mapping strategy. The Character Web shows character development, or events and choices leading to the solution of the character's problem, or randomly organized traits and feelings with connected examples. For both Character Webs and Character Comparisons, the thinking proceeds from concrete to abstract (Example→Idea) and from abstract to concrete (Idea→Example). Unless a list of traits or feelings is used, all the thinking proceeds first from concrete to abstract (Example→Idea).

The Character Comparison ThinkLink requires students to use their experience with Character Webs to discover similarities and/or differences between two or more characters. Since analogy making is a complex process, the teacher may want to delay the introduction of this variety of Character ThinkLink until initial kinds of Event, Theme, and Story ThinkLinks have been taught.

With this character analysis, students are learning a comprehension process to derive personal meaning from reading. Thereby, they are led to the heart of literature.

Chapter 2

The Event ThinkLink

The Event ThinkLink has an event, relationship, problem/solution, or choice as the central focus. Events are moments, brief scenes, or extended action, and are analyzed for thematic content, causes and effects, and for similarity to other events. Hence, there are three varieties of the Event ThinkLink: Event-Idea, Event-Cause/Effect, and the Event-Analogy.

THE EVENT-IDEA THINKLINK

Definition and Prototype

One variety of the Event ThinkLink is the Event-Idea ThinkLink in which an idea or ideas are abstracted from events, relationships, story problems/solutions, or choices. These ideas include character traits/feelings, story themes, and causes or effects. The definition of theme is found in the Glossary on page 98, and a list of themes is found in the Appendix on page 78. A list of traits/feelings is found in the Appendix on pages 75 through 77. The following prototype shows the basic linking from event to ideas.

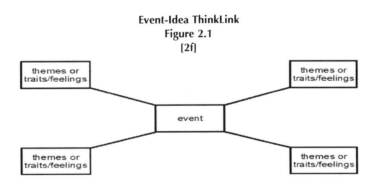

Event-Idea ThinkLink
Figure 2.1
[2f]

Instruction

The teacher prepares for the Event-Idea ThinkLink by demonstrating how to derive traits/feelings or ideas from an event, relationship, or story problem/solution in life or literature. For instance, the final parade scene of *The Emperor's New Clothes* might yield fear, lying, exposure, peer pressure, and self-deception. Over time, once students are able to reason in this manner, from Example→Idea, they are ready for guided practice in the Event-Idea ThinkLink. Examples that show some possibilities are found in Figures 2.2 through 2.4.

Event-Idea ThinkLink
Figure 2.2
[2f]

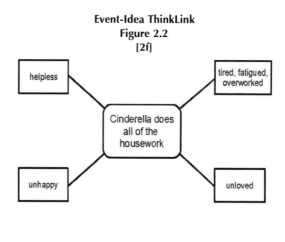

Event-Idea ThinkLink
Figure 2.3
[2f]

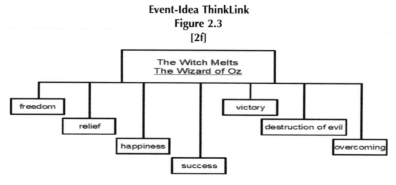

Figure 2.4 is an example of an Event-Idea Analogy combination, actually a composite of events. Most of the ThinkLink samples shown throughout this book could accommodate different thinking types. The discovery of these various combinations is a reinforcing experience for students and teachers.

Event-Idea ThinkLink
Figure 2.4
[2c, 2f]

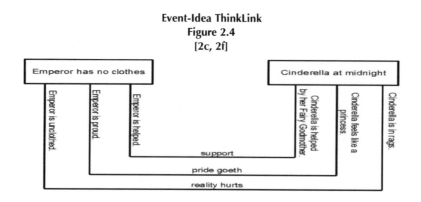

EVENT-CAUSE/EFFECT THINKLINK

Definition and Prototypes

Another variety of the Event ThinkLink is the Event-Cause/Effect ThinkLink that shows how some events, relationships, story problems/solutions, or important choices lead to or are the result of other events or ideas within the plot of the story. In the following prototypes, Figures 2.5 through 2.7, although the direction of the arrows indicates that the cause leads to effect, the thinking process sometimes begins with an effect.

Event-Cause/Effect ThinkLink
Figure 2.5
[2b]

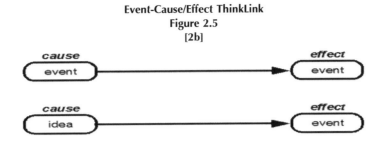

Event-Cause/Effect ThinkLink
Figure 2.6
[2b]

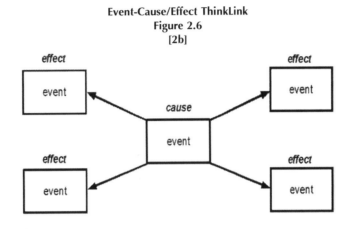

Event-Cause/Effect ThinkLink
Figure 2.7
[2b]

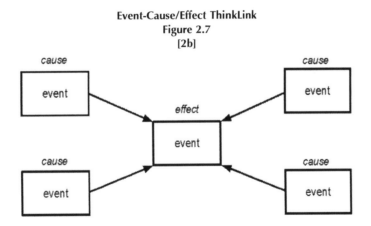

Instruction

To begin the *Demonstration and Guided Practice Stage* with a small or large group, the teacher charts, as a model, single Event-Cause/Effect ThinkLinks. The examples are sometimes derived from the students' life experiences. Initially, Event-Cause/Effect ThinkLinks are charted where either the cause is given and the effect is to be found, or the effect is given and the cause is to be found. The following are skeletal ThinkLinks that the teacher uses for guided practice. For younger students particularly, partially completed Skeletal Webs provide the necessary structure. In Figures 2.8 through 2.11, the parentheses indicate a response that the student needs to find. This part of the *Demonstration and Guided Practice Stage* is totally teacher-directed with student responses charted by the teacher.

Event-Cause/Effect ThinkLink
Figure 2.8
[2b]

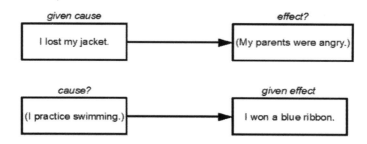

given cause   *effect?*

I lost my jacket. ──────────▶ (My parents were angry.)

cause?   *given effect*

(I practice swimming.) ──────────▶ I won a blue ribbon.

Event-Cause/Effect ThinkLink
Figure 2.9
[2b]

given cause   *effect?*

Dorothy uses the slippers. ──────────▶ (The witch melts.)

Event-Cause/Effect ThinkLink
Figure 2.10
[2b]

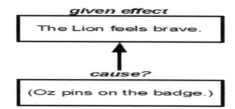

given effect

The Lion feels brave.

▲

cause?

(Oz pins on the badge.)

Event-Cause/Effect ThinkLink
Figure 2.11
[2b]

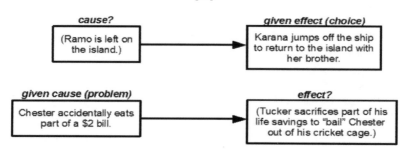

cause?   *given effect (choice)*

(Ramo is left on the island.) ──────────▶ Karana jumps off the ship to return to the island with her brother.

given cause (problem)   *effect?*

Chester accidentally eats part of a $2 bill. ──────────▶ (Tucker sacrifices part of his life savings to "bail" Chester out of his cricket cage.)

Once the single cause, single effect concept is understood, the teacher continues the *Demonstration and Guided Practice* with multiple Cause/Effect ThinkLinks. When the teacher charts the ThinkLinks, either the cause is given and effects are found or the effect is given and the causes are found, as shown in Figures 2.12 through 2.15.

Event-Cause/Effect ThinkLink
Figure 2.12
[2b]

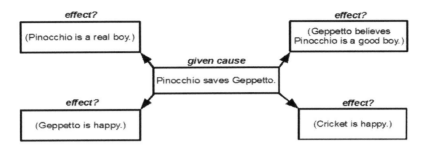

Event-Cause/Effect ThinkLink
Figure 2.13
[2b]

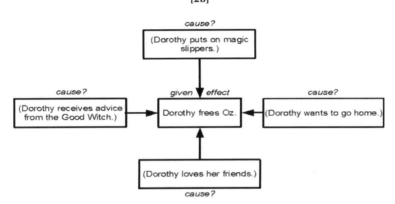

Event-Cause/Effect ThinkLink
Figure 2.14
[2b]

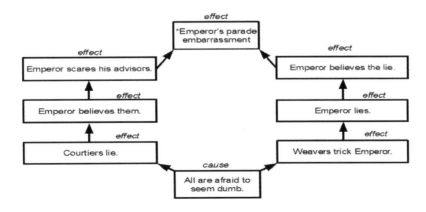

In Figure 2.14, start with the given ultimate effect and proceed to the major cause. Then follow the two lines of the effects to the ultimate effect.

Event-Cause/Effect ThinkLink
Figure 2.15
[2b]

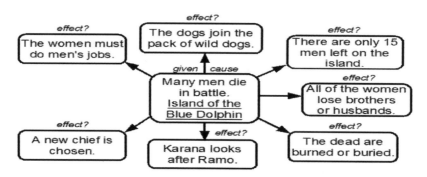

After sufficient teacher-directed charting of the Event-Cause/Effect ThinkLinks, students are ready to complete additional ThinkLinks to further analyze the story plot. When the Event-Cause/Effect ThinkLinks are used to further analyze the story plot, then significant events embodying the main character's problem(s)*/solution(s) and important choice(s) need to be considered. If the given effect is a character's problem or choice, the students then map causal events leading to the problem or choice. The character's problem or choice may have effects that also can be mapped. If the given effect is the solution to the character's problem, then the students determine important causal events leading to that problem/solution, as shown in the prototypes in Figures 2.16 through 2.23. During the *Demonstration and Guided Practice Stage*, the teacher often provides the problem(s)/solutions(s) or choice events, as shown in Figures 2.20 through 2.23.

Event-Cause/Effect ThinkLink
Figure 2.16
[2b]

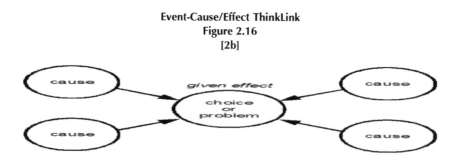

*Whereas the problem is not in the strictest sense an event, its analysis requires dealing with events.

Event-Cause/Effect ThinkLink
Figure 2.17
[2b]

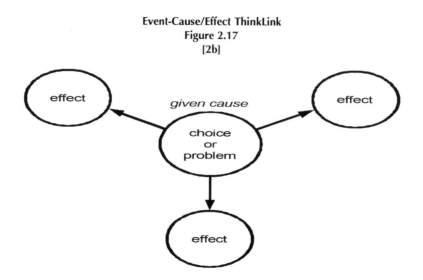

Event-Cause/Effect ThinkLink
Figure 2.18
[2b]

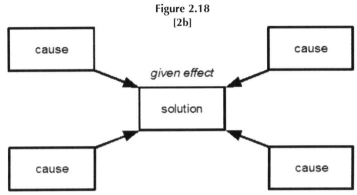

Event-Cause/Effect ThinkLink
Figure 2.19
[2b]

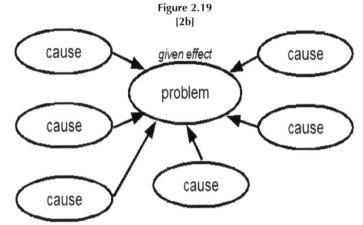

Event-Cause/Effect ThinkLink
Figure 2.20
[2b]

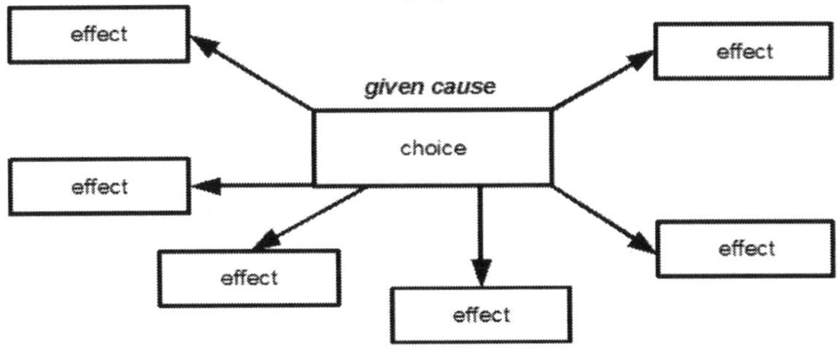

Event-Cause/Effect ThinkLink
Figure 2.21
[2b]

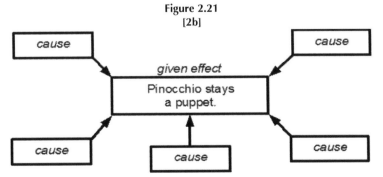

Event-Cause/Effect ThinkLink
Figure 2.22
[2b]

Event-Cause/Effect ThinkLink
Figure 2.23
[2b]

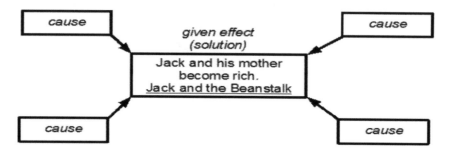

Event-Cause/Effect ThinkLink
Figure 2.24
[2b]

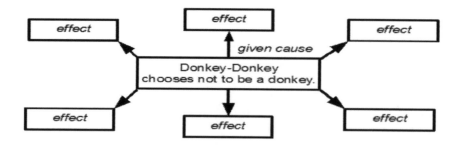

During the *Independent Production Stage* the students create their own Event-Cause/Effect ThinkLinks with or without the teacher's given point of departure. With experienced primary or intermediate students, it is not always necessary for the teacher to supply causes or effects; that is, to ask specific questions. For example, the teacher directs the students to choose an event, relationship, story problem/solution, or character choice; pick a ThinkLink shape; and construct the Event-Cause/Effect ThinkLink.

Once again, when students are mapping, it is very important for them to choose significant events such as the problem/solution or important choice in order to show an in-depth analysis of the story plot and the characters, as shown in Figures 2.25 through 2.27.

Event-Cause/Effect ThinkLink
Figure 2.25
[2b]

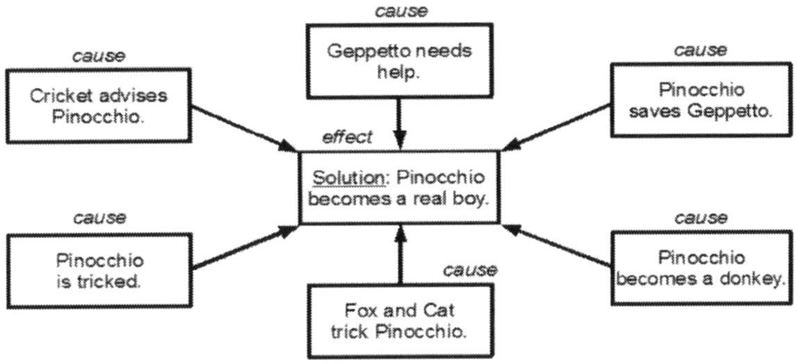

cause

Geppetto needs help.

cause

Cricket advises Pinocchio.

cause

Pinocchio saves Geppetto.

effect

Solution: Pinocchio becomes a real boy.

cause

Pinocchio is tricked.

cause

Fox and Cat trick Pinocchio.

cause

Pinocchio becomes a donkey.

Event-Cause/Effect ThinkLink
Figure 2.26
[2b]

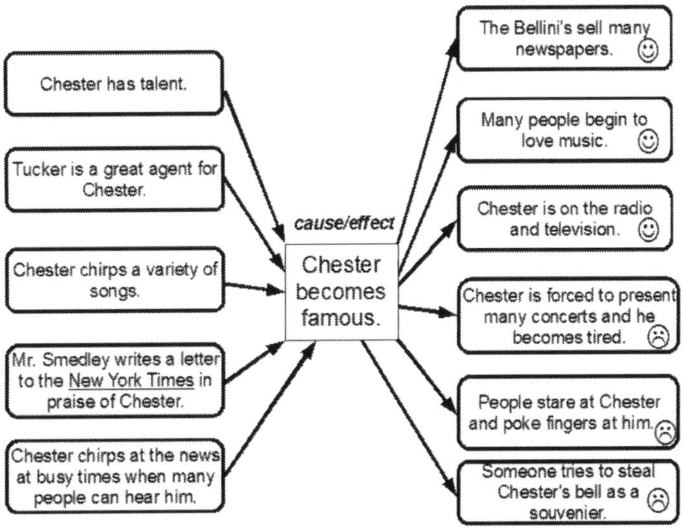

Chester has talent.

Tucker is a great agent for Chester.

Chester chirps a variety of songs.

Mr. Smedley writes a letter to the <u>New York Times</u> in praise of Chester.

Chester chirps at the news at busy times when many people can hear him.

cause/effect

Chester becomes famous.

The Bellini's sell many newspapers. ☺

Many people begin to love music. ☺

Chester is on the radio and television. ☺

Chester is forced to present many concerts and he becomes tired. ☹

People stare at Chester and poke fingers at him. ☹

Someone tries to steal Chester's bell as a souvenier. ☹

Event-Cause/Effect ThinkLink
Figure 2.27
[2e]

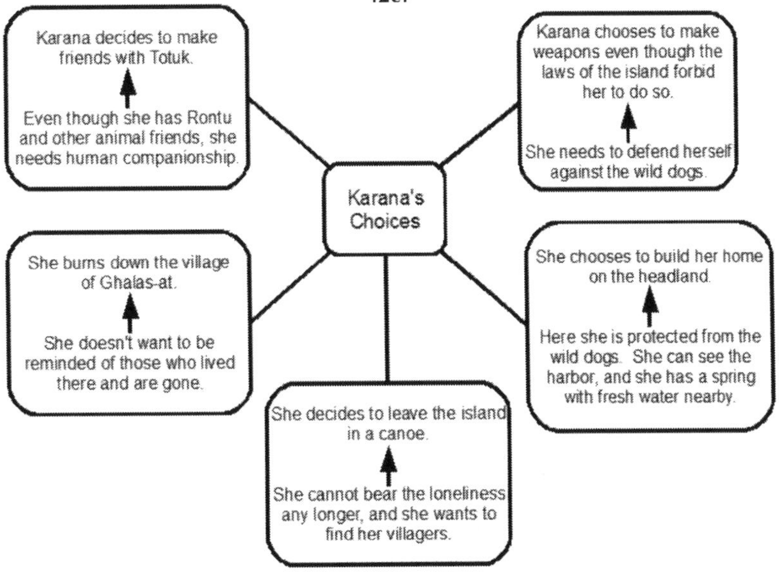

Karana decides to make friends with Totuk.

Even though she has Rontu and other animal friends, she needs human companionship.

Karana chooses to make weapons even though the laws of the island forbid her to do so.

She needs to defend herself against the wild dogs.

Karana's Choices

She burns down the village of Ghalas-at.

She doesn't want to be reminded of those who lived there and are gone.

She chooses to build her home on the headland.

Here she is protected from the wild dogs. She can see the harbor, and she has a spring with fresh water nearby.

She decides to leave the island in a canoe.

She cannot bear the loneliness any longer, and she wants to find her villagers.

THE EVENT-ANALOGY THINKLINK

Definition and Prototypes

A third variety of the Event ThinkLink incorporates analogy. Events are compared to other events to determine similar traits/feelings or themes, common significance in the plot, and similar causes or effects. Prototypes of single and multiple Event-Analogy ThinkLinks follow.

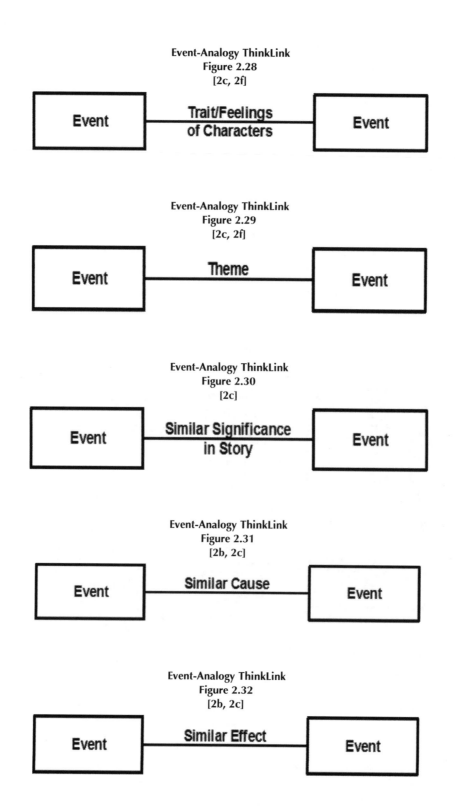

Event-Analogy ThinkLink
Figure 2.28
[2c, 2f]

Event — Trait/Feelings of Characters — Event

Event-Analogy ThinkLink
Figure 2.29
[2c, 2f]

Event — Theme — Event

Event-Analogy ThinkLink
Figure 2.30
[2c]

Event — Similar Significance in Story — Event

Event-Analogy ThinkLink
Figure 2.31
[2b, 2c]

Event — Similar Cause — Event

Event-Analogy ThinkLink
Figure 2.32
[2b, 2c]

Event — Similar Effect — Event

Event-Analogy ThinkLink
Figure 2.33
[2c, 2f]

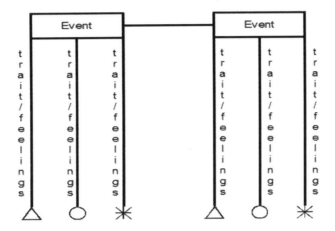

Event-Analogy ThinkLink
Figure 2.34
[2c, 2f]

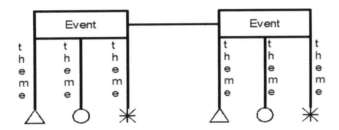

Event-Analogy ThinkLink
Figure 2.35
[2b, 2c]

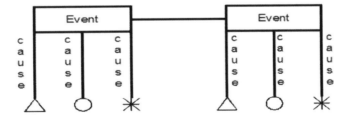

Event-Analogy ThinkLink
Figure 2.36
[2b, 2c]

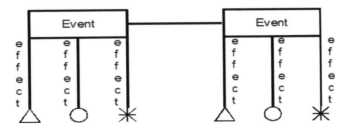

Instruction

When students have had experience comparing characters, event-to-event comparisons become a familiar task. Although character comparisons sometimes include differences, event comparisons generally focus on similarities. Instruction begins with the teacher demonstrating single element analogies from literature and life, as shown in the prototypes in Figures 2.28 through 2.31. Once students have produced these ThinkLinks, they move through the instructional stages with the multielement analogies of the same variety, as shown in the prototypes in Figures 2.32 through 2.37.

Event-Analogy ThinkLink
Figure 2.37
[2b, 2c, 2f]

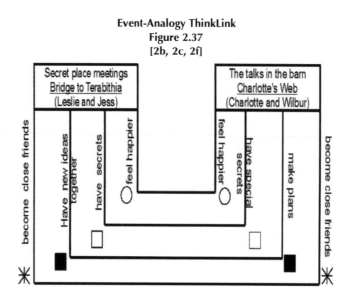

Event-Analogy ThinkLink
Figure 2.38
[2c, 2f]

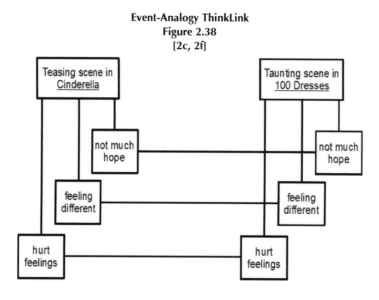

SUMMARY

There are three varieties of the Event ThinkLink—the Event-Idea, the Event-Cause/Effect, and the Event-Analogy. Events are considered moments, brief scenes, extended action, relationships, problems/solutions, or choices that are analyzed for thematic content, causes and effects, and similarity to other events. Responding to life and literature by focusing on events allows the students to think from the most concrete departure point; hence, Event ThinkLinks are a possible beginning point for the ThinkLink metacognitive mapping strategy. As students work, they recognize and refer frequently to the types of thinking they are doing.

Chapter 3

The Theme ThinkLink

The Theme ThinkLink that focuses on story themes is another kind of ThinkLink useful in deepening the analysis of stories. A theme is an idea that weaves throughout parts of the story or the entire story. Stories have major and minor themes, as well as other ideas not recurrent enough to be considered themes. These lesser ideas may also be the focus of thinking. Relationships and problems/solutions, though often considered examples, are sometimes focal points for the Theme ThinkLink.

THE THEME-EXAMPLE THINKLINK

Definition and Prototypes

One variety of the Theme ThinkLink is a Theme-Example ThinkLink in which examples of the theme are found within one story or in several stories. Examples embodying the theme could be events, relationships, story problems/solutions, or other stories. The following are prototypes of Theme-Example ThinkLinks, as shown in Figures 3.1 through 3.3.

Theme-Example ThinkLink
Figure 3.1
[3e]

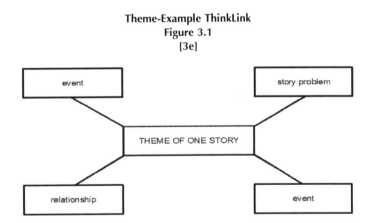

Theme-Example ThinkLink
Figure 3.2
[3e]

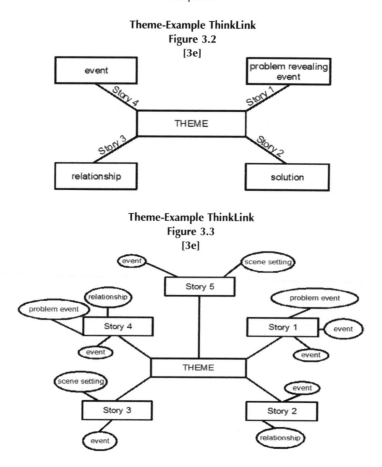

Theme-Example ThinkLink
Figure 3.3
[3e]

Instruction

Before actual instruction begins, the teacher demonstrates how to derive ideas from events, or classify events, in stories, as shown in Chapter 2, pages 36 and 37. The students then derive their own ideas and these are listed and displayed. From a list of familiar stories such as that found in the Appendix on pages 73 and 74, further examples of each idea are generated, and the meanings are discussed. Then the teacher teaches the concept of theme as a recurring idea by finding several events, relationships, or problems/solutions that exemplify the theme in one story. The complexity and the wording of the ideas and themes found in the Appendix on page 78 vary according to the students' developmental levels. Prior work done with deriving feelings and traits of characters is preparation for this activity.

When introducing the Theme-Example ThinkLink, the teacher and/or students derive a major theme from similar events in one story. Using this single story as a context, the students then supply the examples—the events, relationships, or problems/solutions from the story that support the theme. The teacher then charts these examples in order of their occurrence within the story or randomly, as shown in Figures 3.4 and 3.5.

After demonstrating a Theme-Example ThinkLink, the teacher continues the process with other stories. The students, working individually or in pairs, then construct ThinkLinks by choosing events, relationships, or problems/solutions within a story to exemplify a major theme, as shown in Figures 3.4 through 3.8.

Theme-Example ThinkLink
Figure 3.4
[3e]

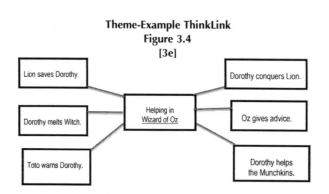

Theme-Example ThinkLink
Figure 3.5
[3e]

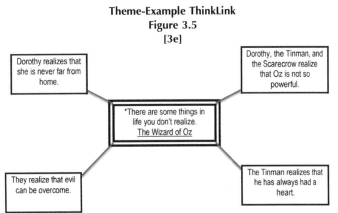

*Two third grade girls in a discussion derived this theme from *The Wonderful Wizard of Oz* in a **Think-Pair-Share** discussion.

Because the choices that characters make are often an important aspect of the story, choice could be considered a theme if the decision-making is crucial to the plot. Students, determining choices in stories, experience in-depth understanding of the major story plot, as shown in Figures 3.7 and 3.8.

Theme-Example ThinkLink
Figure 3.6
[3e]

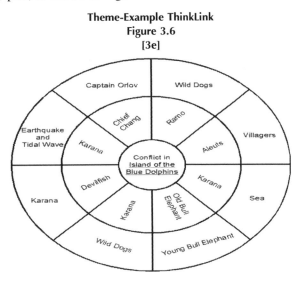

Most ThinkLinks can be shaped as concentric circles. Figure 3.6 places the characters that are in conflict in the same segment but in a separate orbit of the circle.

Theme-Example ThinkLink
Figure 3.7
[3e]

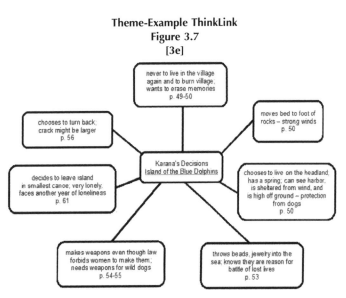

In this context, Karana's decision-making is considered a theme because of its centrality.

Theme-Example ThinkLink
Figure 3.8
[3e]

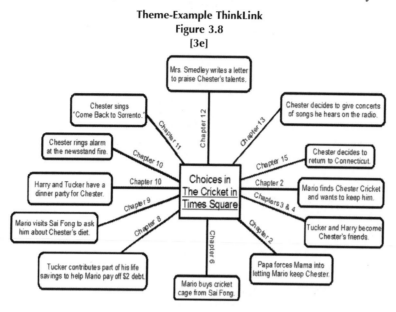

When students understand the concept of theme and have worked with a single context, or one story, they are ready to exemplify a theme by citing events, relationships, or problems/solutions from multicontext or from several stories. It is from this multicontext activity that the students gain the fullest understanding of the concept of theme and come upon some of the *big ideas* in life. The teacher constructs and discusses with the students a Theme Example ThinkLink using examples from various stories. The theme need not be the major theme of each story. A wall-cued or personal list of familiar stories, such as those found in the Appendix on pages 73 and 74, aids this process. Figures 3.9 through 3.12 are shaped as webs, wheels, or a concentric hexagon.

Theme-Example ThinkLink
Figure 3.9
[3c, 3e]

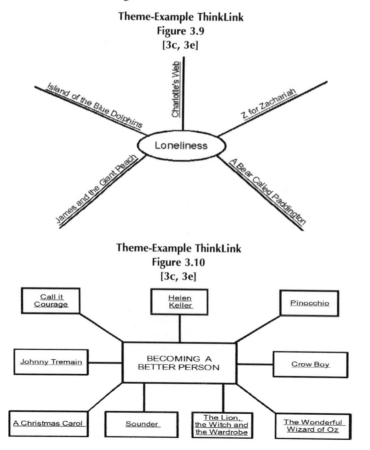

Theme-Example ThinkLink
Figure 3.10
[3c, 3e]

Theme-Example ThinkLink
Figure 3.11
[3c, 3e]

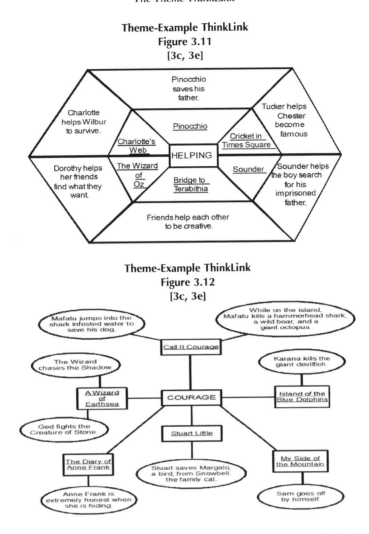

Theme-Example ThinkLink
Figure 3.12
[3c, 3e]

Intermediate or advanced primary students are able to work at the complexity level of a ThinkLink, as in Figure 3.13, in which the theme is quite general and in which the examples yield a more specific theme. In Figures 3.14 and 3.15, the examples are relationships, and the examples yield characteristics of a theme. This more complex map gives a hint of the variations possible with the ThinkLink metacognitive mapping strategy and is a good example of a blueprint for a written composition, as shown on pages 89 through 96.

Figure 3.16 is a Theme-Theme-Example ThinkLink in which characteristics of the theme are explored in one context and then related by analogy to other contexts. Story lists are crucial for this activity, as shown on pages 73 and 74. The students working at this overall level of complexity are preparing for the Theme Cause/Effect ThinkLink.

Theme-Example ThinkLink
Figure 3.13
[3c, 3e]

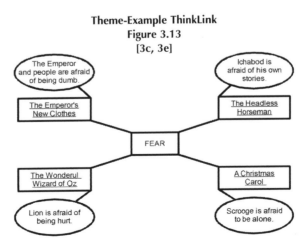

Theme-Example ThinkLink
Figure 3.14
[3c, 3e, 3f]

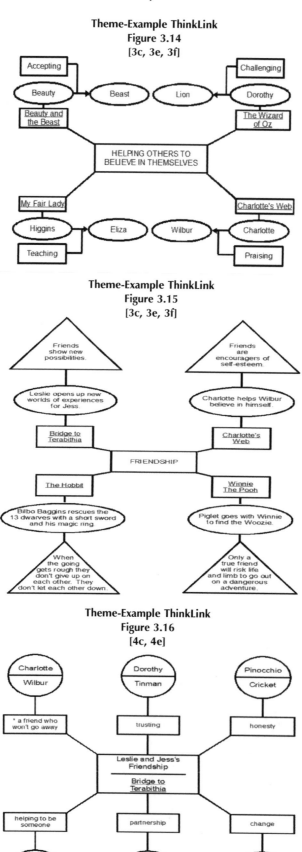

Theme-Example ThinkLink
Figure 3.15
[3c, 3e, 3f]

Theme-Example ThinkLink
Figure 3.16
[4c, 4e]

*A fourth grade student derived this theme during a group discussion.

THE THEME-CAUSE/EFFECT THINKLINK

Definition and Prototypes

A second variety of the Theme ThinkLink is the Theme-Cause/Effect ThinkLink. Using theme as a departure point, experiences in literature or life are analyzed for causes or effects. The Theme-Cause/Effect ThinkLink has two variations: specific, in which a question is answered within one story, or a single context; and general, in which a question is answered by analogy from many stories, or multicontext. Figures 3.17 through 3.20 illustrate the single context Theme-Cause/Effect ThinkLink and Figures 3.21 and 3.22 illustrate the multicontext Theme-Cause/Effect ThinkLink.

Theme is sometimes the label for a central story problem. For example, "losing direction" is a theme in *Pinocchio*. It is also a rendering of a central problem of the story.

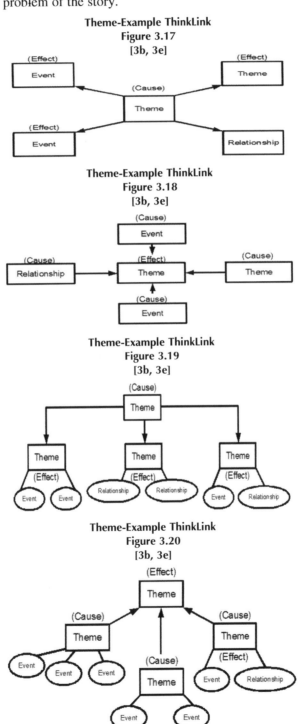

Theme-Example ThinkLink
Figure 3.17
[3b, 3e]

Theme-Example ThinkLink
Figure 3.18
[3b, 3e]

Theme-Example ThinkLink
Figure 3.19
[3b, 3e]

Theme-Example ThinkLink
Figure 3.20
[3b, 3e]

Theme-Example ThinkLink
Figure 3.21
[3b, 3c, 3e, 3f]

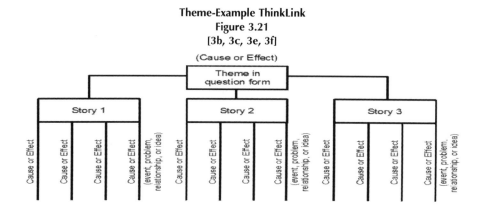

Theme-Example ThinkLink
Figure 3.22
[3b, 3c, 3e]

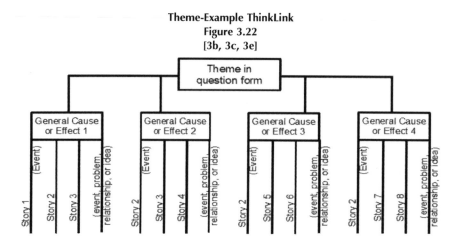

Instruction

Initially, during the Demonstration and Practice Stage, cause or effect thematic questions are answered from a specific story, or one context: "What are the effects of Charlotte's helping in *Charlotte's Web*? What are the causes of the embarrassment of the Emperor in his new clothes?" In this case, answers are written in terms of events, relationships, problems, ideas, sometimes themes, and traits/feelings, as shown in Figures 3.23 through 3.25.

After students independently map the Theme-Cause/Effect ThinkLink using one context, the teacher begins the demonstration of the general or multicontext Theme-Cause/Effect ThinkLink. A question relevant to students is derived from a theme, or an interesting question is chosen from a listing of questions designed to probe the themes or ideas, as shown in the Appendix on pages 79 through 82. For example, for the theme change, the question could be "How can a person help another person change for the better?"

There are two ways to answer the question with a ThinkLink: one in which stories or events are analyzed for causes and effects—in this case, causes, and similar causes and effects are connected or coded, as shown in Figures 3.26 and 3.27; and another way, in which general causes and effects are derived immediately and stories or events sought to substantiate, as shown in Figure 3.28. The first way is Idea→Example→Idea, or specific to general organization; and the second is Idea→Idea→Example, or general to specific organization. In both cases, of course, the original reasoning is from Example→Idea because to derive the idea, students need to know the examples.

Instruction in this general multicontext Theme-Cause/Effect ThinkLink, "What are the effects of helping others?" is complicated and requires in-depth modeling, demonstration, and practice, as found on pages 89 through 93. This Think-Link necessitates a survey of a number of sources from literature, drama, and life experience. Therefore, to aid the memory, the cueing of stories, character traits/feelings, and themes is suggested, as in the Appendix on pages 73 through 78.

Theme-Example ThinkLink
Figure 3.23
[3b, 3f]

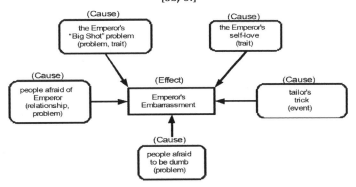

Theme-Example ThinkLink
Figure 3.24
[3b, 3f]

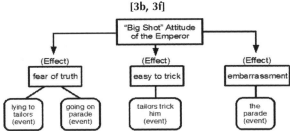

Theme-Example ThinkLink
Figure 3.25
[3b, 3e]

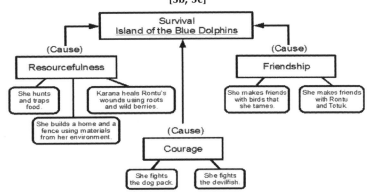

Theme-Example ThinkLink
Figure 3.26
[3b, 3c, 3e, 3f]

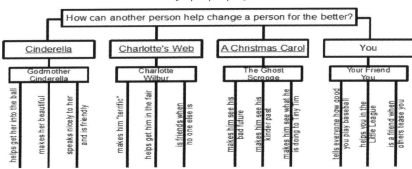

Theme-Example ThinkLink
Figure 3.27
[3b, 3c, 3e, 3f]

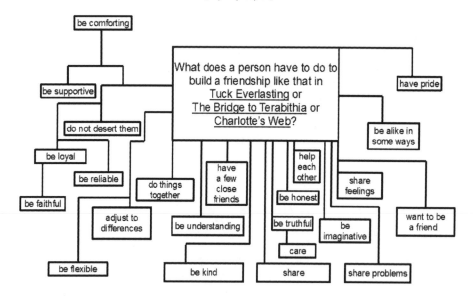

Theme-Example ThinkLink
Figure 3.28
[3b, 3c, 3e]

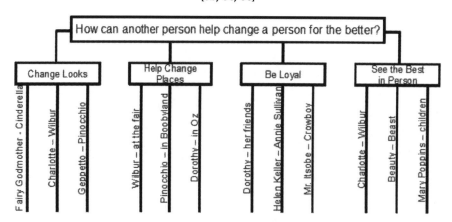

Instruction in the Demonstration and Practice Stage should last long enough that the process becomes second nature to the students. If primary students are involved, most of them probably will do the specific, or single context, Theme-Cause/Effect ThinkLink using the web, wheel, or dangling box shapes. For advanced primary and intermediate students, the multicontext general Theme-Cause/Effect ThinkLink is the high point of the entire ThinkLink metacognitive mapping strategy. It is an experience in theorizing, since general causes or effects are hypothesized.

Once they understand and control the two ways to answer and map a general, or multicontext, cause or effect question, the way to coherent written and oral analytical composition is open to them. The ThinkLink may be used as a blueprint for speaking or writing. The blueprint function is possible for any kind, variety, or form of ThinkLink. Reading becomes an opportunity for asking and responding to life's major questions.

In the Independent Production Stage, the teacher encourages the students to ask their own questions, invent or choose different ThinkLink shapes, use color coding, use their own lives as a context, survey literature for examples, and convert some of the ThinkLinks into oral or written composition. In the area of oral communication, it is even possible for the students to discuss and act out scenes that reveal the ideas and examples in the ThinkLinks. When this acting-out process is accomplished, the students gain a degree of in-depth understanding of crafted thought rarely attained by other means.

SUMMARY

There are two major varieties of the Theme ThinkLinks—the Theme-Example and the Theme-Cause/Effect. The teaching and student production of both require facility with deriving abstractions, or classifying, and connecting these to concrete examples. Whereas the process involved with Theme-Example ThinkLinks is familiar to students who have done Character and Event ThinkLinks, the Theme-Cause/Effect ThinkLink process is less familiar and more complex. Facility with this latter process in its multi-context analogy signals that students have a high degree of control of the generation, organization, and awareness of thought.

Chapter 4

The Story ThinkLink

For the Story ThinkLink, a story is the point of departure. This open-ended kind embodies essentially the same thinking types as do the Character, Event, and Theme ThinkLinks, though cause/effect is generally not used.

THE STORY-EXAMPLE-IDEA THINKLINK

Definition and Prototypes

One variety of the Story ThinkLink is the Story-Example-Idea ThinkLink or the Story-Idea-Example ThinkLink in which one story is the central focus. Figures 4.1 through 4.3 are prototypes shaped in various ways, and, as is the case with the other ThinkLink kinds/varieties, many other shapes are possible, as shown on pages xiii through xiv. It is important to note here that examples in the story refer to events, relationships, and story problems/solutions, and that ideas are sometimes pervasive enough to be themes.

Story-Example-Idea ThinkLink
Figure 4.1
[4f]

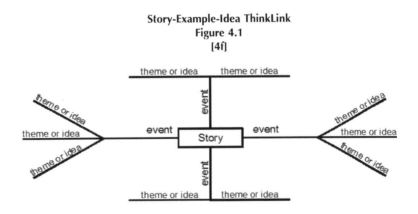

Story-Idea-Example Idea ThinkLink
Figure 4.2
[4e]

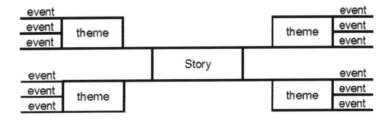

Story-Idea-Example Idea ThinkLink
Figure 4.3
[4e]

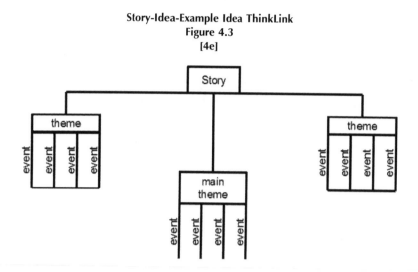

Instruction

The Story-Example-Idea ThinkLink is taught first because it is easier to derive the abstraction or classification from specific examples such as events, relationships, and problems/solutions than it is from an entire story, as shown in Figures 4.1 through 4.3. Since there is an obvious similarity in thinking between the Story ThinkLink and the Event ThinkLink, much of the preparation for the Story-Example-Idea ThinkLink can be achieved through teacher and students together deriving ideas or themes from events or other examples, as found in the Appendix on page 78.

When students are able to abstract ideas from examples, or to classify examples, and when many ideas have been derived, the teacher demonstrates the use of an entire story as a source. To simplify this process, the teacher may use a list of ideas or themes already derived to look for the most important ideas or themes. For this demonstration, nursery rhymes, fables, and fairy tales are good starters, and students enjoy wording themes as morals or proverbs. Figures 4.4 and 4.5 illustrate this concept.

Story-Idea-Example Idea ThinkLink
Figure 4.4
[4f]

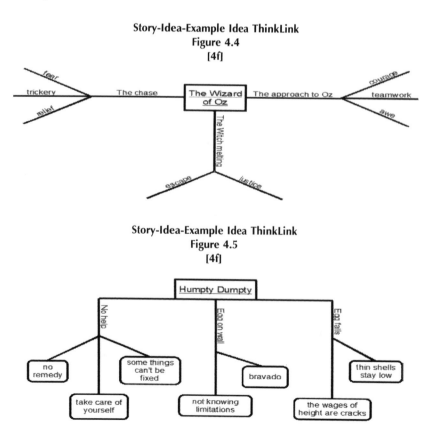

Story-Idea-Example Idea ThinkLink
Figure 4.5
[4f]

The Story-Idea-Example ThinkLink is generally difficult for primary students because in order to derive abstractions, they must first consciously think of specific events, relationships, or problems from the story. For instance, when selecting a main theme of *The Wonderful Wizard of Oz*, it helps to first think of crucial events and the actions of central characters.

The best preparation for the more difficult process of going from the story directly to deriving, exemplifying, and mapping ideas is prior experience, teacher demonstration, and guided practice. This complex process of deriving themes or ideas directly from the whole story is illustrated in Figures 4.6 and 4.7. Whereas students are reasoning from Example→Idea, they are not consciously aware of the examples. It is important that the teacher makes it clear to students that they are making their own meaning from the story and, hence, may derive different ideas or main themes.

Story-Idea-Example Idea ThinkLink
Figure 4.6
[4e]

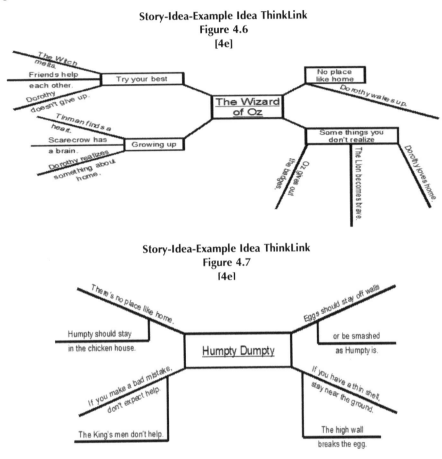

Story-Idea-Example Idea ThinkLink
Figure 4.7
[4e]

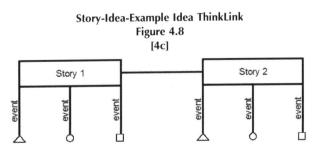

THE STORY-ANALOGY THINKLINK

Definition and Prototypes

Another variety of Story ThinkLink is the Story-Analogy ThinkLink in which two or more stories are compared to determine similar events and story elements such as setting, problems/solutions, characterization, style of writing, or themes. Figures 4.8 through 4.15 are prototypes. This variety of ThinkLink is an ideal blueprint strategy for written comparative analysis of books.

Story-Idea-Example Idea ThinkLink
Figure 4.8
[4c]

Story-Idea-Example Idea ThinkLink
Figure 4.9
[4c]

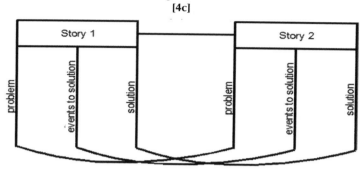

Story-Element-Analogy ThinkLink
Figure 4.10
[4c]

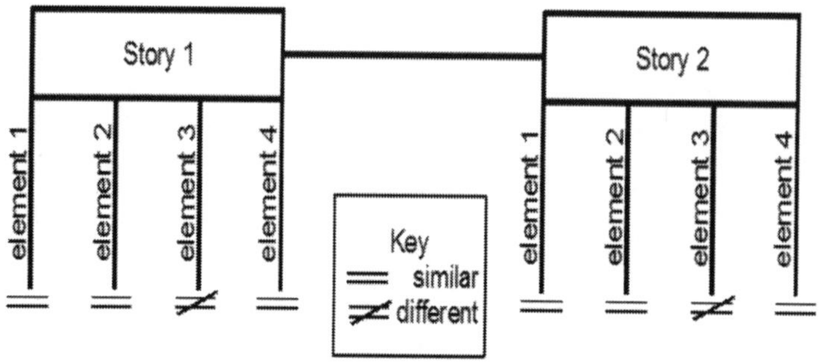

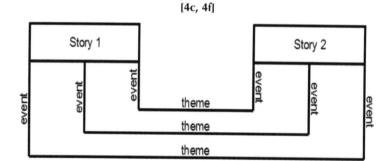

Story-Element-Analogy ThinkLink
Figure 4.11
[4c, 4f]

Story-Element-Analogy ThinkLink
Figure 4.12
[4c, 4e, 4f]

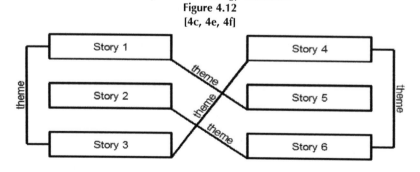

Story-Theme-Analogy ThinkLink
Figure 4.13
[4c, 4e, 4f]

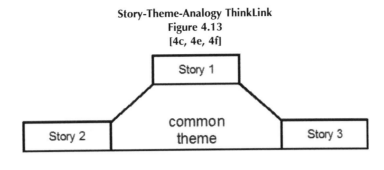

Story-Theme-Analogy ThinkLink
Figure 4.14
[4c, 4e, 4f]

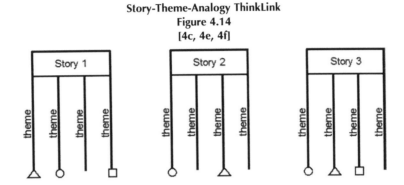

Story-Theme-Stories-Analogy ThinkLink
Figure 4.15
[4c, 4e, 4f]

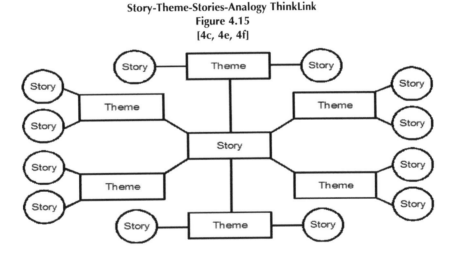

Instruction

As with all analogy making, it is imperative that sufficient memory cues of other contexts be available, as found in the Appendix on pages 73 and 74. It is also important that students understand that there are many possible responses and many ThinkLink shapes to express them. These forms are cued on the wall, as shown on pages xiii through xiv. Some primary students find analogical thinking difficult, and either will not be able to do story analogy, or should at least have considerable practice with character and event analogies first.

For advanced primary or intermediate students, the most independent stage is reached when they explain how themes from different stories are similar or different, as shown in Figures 4.20 and 4.21. At this stage, they independently choose stories and derive themes, sometimes choosing or creating new shapes, color, symbol coding systems, and artistic embellishments for the ThinkLinks. Figures 4.16 through 4.24 illustrate some of these variations.

Story-Event-Analogy ThinkLink
Figure 4.16
[4c]

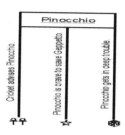

Story-Problem/Solution-Analogy ThinkLink
Figure 4.17
[4c]

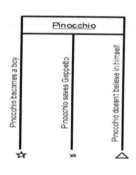

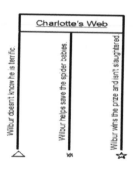

Story-Problem-Analogy ThinkLink
Figure 4.18
[4c, 4e, 4f]

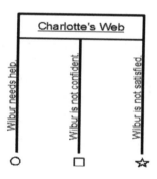

Story-Element-Analogy ThinkLink
Figure 4.19
[4c, 4e, 4f]

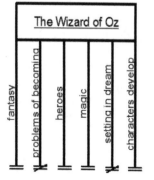

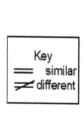

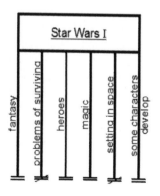

Story-Element-Theme-Analogy ThinkLink
Figure 4.20
[4c, 4e, 4f]

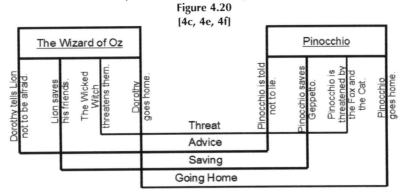

Story-Event-Theme-Analogy ThinkLink
Figure 4.21
[4c, 4e, 4f]

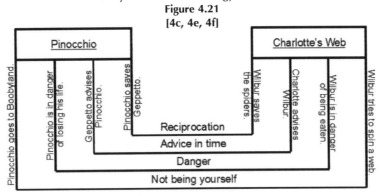

Story-Theme-Analogy ThinkLink
Figure 4.22
[4c, 4e, 4f]

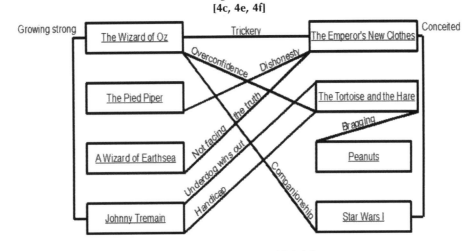

Story-Theme-Analogy ThinkLink
Figure 4.23
[4c, 4e, 4f]

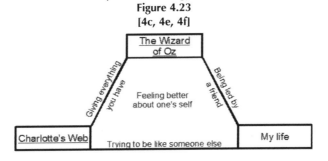

Story-Theme-Analogy ThinkLink
Figure 4.24
[4c, 4e, 4f]

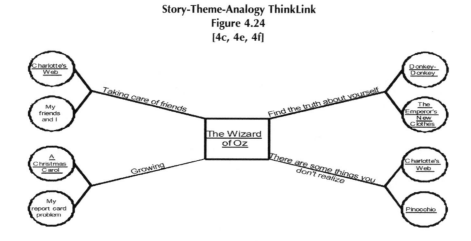

SUMMARY

There are two varieties of the Story ThinkLink—the Story-Example-Idea/Story-Idea-Example, and the Story-Analogy. The procedures and logic for working with this Story kind are essentially the same as for the other three kinds, although there is generally no cause/effect reasoning involved. The Story-Example-Idea/Story-Idea-Example variety is particularly valuable for abstracting the essential themes of a story. The Story-Analogy ThinkLink is also used as the organizer for an in-depth comparative analysis of stories or books and is often a blueprint for written composition. Students can decide for themselves how they are going to compare the stories.

Conclusion

The Shaping of Thought: A Teacher's Guide to Metacognitive Mapping and Critical Thinking in Response to Literature is fundamentally a book about understanding through connections. The combination of ThinkLinks and ThinkTrix create a metacognitive mapping strategy that is central to an engaged classroom of every-student-response and cooperative inquiry, in which all students can find and express meaning from what they read. The four major sections of the book—Character, Event, Theme, and Story—are an organizing framework for the strategy but are not meant to be completely prescriptive.

Teachers using this book can adapt the strategy and its allied components to the realities of their classrooms. The ThinkLink Classroom will have variations but will always be about motivating and empowering the learner. Central to the success of this goal is a teacher, determined that students make sense of literature and their lives. The following *Kaleidoscope of Learning* anchors the ThinkLink metacognitive mapping strategy to the true purposes of education.

The Kaleidoscope of Learning

"Each student is" is an attempt to capture the kaleidoscopic purposes of education. The ThinkLink Classroom is the strategic means to these ends. There are myriad reasons and ways to learn and teach. Students are kaleidoscopic in their needs, abilities, and choices. Each shake of the kaleidoscope and resulting patterns shows a different aspect of each student. The essential message of this book is to be found in the patterns.

Each student is:

a poet
a choice maker
a player with words
a seeker after relatedness, analogy
a unifier
a role player
a reader
a problem solver
a decision-maker
an organizer with a task
a leader
an intrinsically motivated student
a specialist in some areas—a successful person someplace and recognizes it
a person who has in-depth experience from which to make choices
a relater of literature to life, to drama
an identifier, an empathizer with others
a hypothesis maker, a theorizer
a curious person, an asker of questions
a devisor of key questions
an understander of how one knows
a person who is a self-motivated speller, proofreader, reading skill improver
an increasingly able tolerator of ambiguity
a tolerator and weigher of different points of view
a self-analyzer
a listener to impulses and ideas and a valuer of them
a believer in the value of word precision
a believer that there are many ways to express an idea, and often more than one answer to a question
a tuner to consequences
a seeker after cause and effect, cognizant of the high probability of multiple cause and effect
a believer in reinforcing the good and creative in others
a recognizer of the mixed motivation in others
a talker and communicator to peers

69

a learner who realizes that one can learn from peers

a believer and participator in humor

a person who is often enough able to separate his/her worth from achievement or lack of it

a seeker after truth through advocacy rather than through debate

a listener

an anthropologist

a recognizer of the commonality of human dilemmas

a person who recognizes his/her own causative power to create situations and influence people, to change things for better or worse

a recognizer of the causes and consequences of stereotyping, scapegoating, and labeling

a person who habitually attempts to foresee the consequences of his/her own actions and analyze the consequences after the fact

a person open to external and internal experience

a driver to say something, to be

a self-evaluator

a user of models to learn

a studier of individuals and a generalizer from the microcosm

a category hopper, a leaper

a diviner of the general from the particular

a mover from the particular to the general to the particular

a user of categories

a searcher after the primary cause

a coiner of ideas

a turner of phrase

a user of graphic cases

a teacher of others

a collector and user of memory techniques-mnemonics

a user of analogy and examples on tests

an investigator into the origins, evolution, and effect of language

a person who recognizes barriers and systematically works to remove them

a documenter

a comprehender of the concept of selective perception

a recognizer of the impediment of fear to growing

an appreciator of the arts

a believer in everyone's potential (consummate faith)

a fitter of the idiom to the community

a dreamer

a seeker after justice

a searcher for the truth

an appreciator of beauty

a believer in personal growth

a believer in oneself as an authentic person

a recognizer of personal complicity

a worker from microcosms

a discoverer of the structure of an idea, phenomenon, or discipline

an unfreezer of frozen perceptions

an active participant, an involved person

a user of problems as points of departure

a delver beyond habits and training

a player with ideas

a haver of ideas

an actor of ideas

a restructurer

a perceiver of unity in the midst of diversity

a creator of beauty and order out of chaos

a perceiver of new combinations and relationships

a person aware of form, shape, color, mood, and their appearance in media, genre, ideas, disciplines

a sustained worker

a self-motivated, a self-starting individual

a participator in drama

a realizer of potentialities

a self-actualizer and expander, extender, developer

a person open to all experience

an admitter of faults and error

an enhancer of others

a perceiver and judger of each happening on its own merits

a person who uses categories but is not enslaved by them

a checker of hypotheses

a task-orienteer

an evaluator within self

a maker of the familiar strange

a hunch maker

an essence seeker

a person who can stand alone

a believer in self-worth

a rememberer of one's success

a believer in another person's potential to be objective

a critic but not a labeler

a reserver of judgment

a finder of problems

a seeker after the essential question

a seer of oneself as a culture evolver—a language and situation changer

a denier of immediate gratification

a balancer of task with concern for others

a creator within structure

a valuer of persistence

a practitioner and practicer of skills

an inquirer into the unusual, the discrepant, the dissonant

a verifier

a connector of ideas

a ponderer of dissenting points of view

a walker in others' shoes

an attender who focuses

a wonderer at the marvels of nature

a weaver who weaves mistakes into learning

an appreciator of nuance

a finder of aesthetics in truth and truth in the arts

a deriver of principles

a perceiver of the utility and beauty in mathematics

a switcher of tired horses in midstream

an **acceptor** of responsibility

a congratulator

a switcher of tired horses in midstream

a team player in cooperative ventures

a blender of form and function

a skeptic of dichotomies

an expert with a specialty

a prizer of the doubt

Appendix

Contained in the Appendix are classroom questions, student responses, learning tools, and activities that reveal the essence of the ThinkLink metacognitive mapping strategy. Careful examination of these materials gives a picture of the scope and depth of the ThinkLink Classroom. Visual organization, or shaping of thought, and shared metacognition, or community knowledge of how the mind works, are the heart of a program that encourages and enables students to find meaning in, and an understanding of, literature and life.

TOOLS AND CUES

List of Familiar Stories

To make connections that are the essence of the ThinkLink Classroom, a wall-charted list of familiar stories is essential. Remembering contexts is essential to the flow of ideas. In addition, each student can have a personal list of stories in a desk tool kit or folder. The list is specific to every classroom. The following selections from fables, fairy tales, films, videos, novels, nursery rhymes, plays, short stories, and television specials are reflective of those used in this book but are by no means inclusive.

A Bear Called Paddington
A Christmas Carol
Alice and Wonderland
Amos and Boris
Amos Fortune, Free Man
A Picture Book of Martin Luther King, Jr.
A Wizard of Earthsea
Beauty and the Beast
Born Free, the film
Bridge to Terabithia
Broderick
Call It Courage
Charlotte's Web
Cinderella
Crow Boy
Donkey-Donkey
100 Dresses
E. T. The Extra-Terrestrial, a novel and the film
Happy Birthday, Martin Luther King
Hatchet
Helen Keller
"Humpty Dumpty"

Hurray for Captain Jane
Island of the Blue Dolphins
Jack and the Beanstalk
James and the Giant Peach
Johnny Tremain
Julie of the Wolves
Little Bear
Lovable Lyle (Lyle the Crocodile)
Martin Luther King, Jr.
Mary Poppins, the novel and the film
Maybe a Mole
Mr. Popper's Penquins
My Fair Lady, a musical play and film
My Side of the Mountain
Peanuts
Peanuts Revisited
Pinocchio
Sounder
Star Wars I, Episode VI, the film
Stuart Little
The Beagle Has Landed
The Black Pearl
The Cricket in Times Square
The Diary of a Young Girl
The Emperor's New Clothes, a fairy tale
It's the Great Pumpkin, Charlie Brown, an animated television special
The Headless Horseman
The Hobbit
The King and I, the play and the film
The Legend of Sleepy Hollow
The Lion, the Witch and the Wardrobe, the first book of the Chronicles of Narnia
The Pied Piper, a legend
The Mixed-Up Files of Mrs. Basil E. Frankweiler
The Secret Box
The Sign of the Beaver
The Sound of Music, an English film
The Tale of Peter Rabbit
The Tales of Uncle Remus
The Tortoise and the Hare, an Aesop fable
The Trumpet of the Swan
The Velveteen Rabbit
The Wonderful Wizard of Oz
Thunder Rolling in the Mountains
Thomasina
Tower by the Sea
Tucker Mouse
Winnie-the-Pooh
You've Come a Long Way, Charlie Brown
Z for Zachariah

CHARACTER TRAITS/FEELINGS

Students derive character traits and feelings from life, literature, and film. These can be charted, though it is a more challenging intellectual task for students to conceptualize and generalize from the story directly. The best use of the list is to take from it an idea and find examples of the idea in the story list. This list comes from actual classrooms, as does nearly every **ThinkLink** sample in this book. Each class can derive its own list from common literature and life experience.

cooperative	positive	humble	ecstatic
affectionate	earnest	dignified	merry
patriotic	adventurous	modest	caring
conscientious	nature-lover	happy-go-lucky	just
thoughtful	eager	creative	gentle
intelligent	faithful	well-mannered	daring
humane	persistent	romantic	serene
observant	satisfied	vigilant	happy
merciful	good-hearted	charitable	noble
healthy	independent	scholarly	alert
optimistic	confident	thrilled	proud
imaginative	enchanting	broad-minded	tidy
friendly	studious	knowledgeable	quiet
ambitious	charming	grateful	true
sharing	dependable	cheerful	busy
determined	diligent	efficient	jolly
inventive	enthusiastic	humorous	loyal
agreeable	relieved	majestic	kind
hopeful	carefree	frolicsome	lucky
supportive	dashing	resourceful	smart
patient	affable	trustworthy	happy
courageous	serious	warm-hearted	brave
talented	honest	successful	clever
surprised	amiable	respectful	adroit
considerate	curious	democratic	secure
artistic	exuberant	tolerant	frugal
outgoing	encouraged	quick-thinking	joyful
responsible	complimentary	enterprising	heroic
musical	amazed	perseverant	bold
dramatic	debonair	idealistic	demure
athletic	well-organized	energetic	strong
self-reliant	peaceful	skillful	polite
careful	jubilant	obedient	elated
jovial	delighted	gracious	loving

helpful	generous	honorable	restful
stately	industrious	compassionate	fair
forgiving	dynamic	sympathetic	reliable
relaxed	dedicated	truthful	valiant
gallant	erudite	courteous	useful

selfish	fearful	bossy	slovenly
uncooperative	snobbish	foolish	sly
thoughtless	frightened	materialistic	wild
disobedient	uncontrolled	arrogant	stern
jealous	insulting	discourteous	vain
envious	frustrated	belligerent	scared
shameless	obnoxious	fierce	tricky
inconsiderate	ill-mannered	mischievous	messy
dependent	ungrateful	big shot	insane
restless	unreliable	horrified	picky
shameful	impatient	pessimistic	tired
irresponsible	insecure	childish	sad
vicious	sarcastic	obsessive	mean
confused	envious	contemptuous	silly
anxious	hopeless	terrified	cruel
quarrelsome	unhappy	unforgiving	shy
blaming	inconsiderate	sneaky	bored
reckless	dependent	tattle-tale	afraid
desperate	worried	deceitful	brutal
discourteous	cowardly	untrustworthy	weak
hateful	discouraged	ignorant	sorry
insulting	indolent	capricious	stingy
argumentative	disgusted	pompous	lazy
impatient	fearless	disorganized	faking
teasing	depressed	bashful	sulky
disrespectful	abandoned	frivolous	angiy
embarrassed	aggressive	infamous	hostile
chaotic	manipulative	disappointed	sickly
hesitant	dishonest	antagonistic	lonely
irritable	impetuous	loud-mouth	crafty
impolite	defiant	unkempt	vulgar
reluctant	nervous	hysterical	unfair
incorrigible	cunning	authoritarian	rude
unscrupulous	indifferent	thoughtless	frantic

stealthy	ostentatious	ferocious	somber
pessimistic	worried	impulsive	whining
careless	despondent	show-off	disgusted
stubborn	uneducated	quick-tempered	greedy
uncooperative	malicious	confused	cranky
daredevil	immoral	defenseless	wicked
unfriendly	incompetent	uneducated	clumsy
negative	thin-skinned	smart-aleck	moody
scornful	temperamental	unsuccessful	cynical
ruthless	forgetful	bossed around	dejected

comical	puzzled	pretending	serious
mysterious	sophisticated	absent-minded	busy
superior	humble	bluffing	grave
doubtful	idealistic	relentless	zealous
dissatisfied	rebellious		

Themes and Ideas

Students identify or develop themes and ideas independently, with each other, and with the teacher. The list here is taken primarily from students. Again, the classroom list is best used to make connections to multiple stories and not to match to one story.

adaptation	helpfulness	partnership	person
faking	injustice	determination	faith in a false god
jealousy	endurance	tenacity	lost chances
revenge	privilege	restraint	rags to riches
freedom	heroism	ridicule	good vs. evil
destruction	resourcefulness	sorcery	top guy
deception	judgment	falsehood	fair weather friend
self-improvement	change	prejudice	change of character
passion	compromise	disillusionment	you in other's eyes
painful friendship	power	charity	some things in life
rebellion	sacrifice	curiosity	you don't realize
independence	realization	sabotage	helping others to
search	cooperation	choice	believe in themselves
unity	humility	discovery	inner conflict
trickery	disappointment	understanding	false promise
liberty	competition	sanctuary	love
overcoming	hopelessness	self-sacrifice	help
handicap	forgiveness	retaliation	fear
attack	loneliness	relief	loss
compassion	salvation	poverty	awe
malevolence	emancipation	false friendship guilt	hope
friendship	success	comedy of errors faith	grief
saving	teamwork	poisoned by mistake	hate
prosperity	perseverance	true love's knot	magic
loyalty	fulfillment	comedy of errors	vanity
redemption	teasing	identity theft	
escape	revolution	king of the hill	
surprise	conformity	appearance and reality	
unconformity	defense	reversal of fortune	
survival	courage	silence is golden	
selfish	giving	one for all, all for one	
caring	temptation	security in numbers	
justice	punishment	haste makes waste	
utopia	sorrow	becoming a better	

Using Questions to Understand Literature and Life

Illustrative samples of student work give an idea of the variety and depth inherent in the strategy. The Cause and Effect questions in this section were developed with and used with intermediate elementary students in Lexington, Massachusetts, and Howard County, Maryland. Students learned how to see similarities and to shape their responses into ThinkLinks from which they talked, dramatized, or wrote cause or effect essays.

THEME	EXAMPLES	CAUSES	EFFECTS
Loneliness	What are some examples of loneliness?	What causes loneliness?	What are the effects of loneliness? What happens when people are lonely?
Friendship	What are some examples of friendship? How do friends treat each other?	How do people become friends? What causes people to become friends? What causes friends to break up?	What does friendship do for people? What are the effects of friendship?
Disabilities	What are some examples of disabilities?	What causes a disability?	What happens when a person an/cannot get over a disability?
Prejudice	What are some causes of prejudice? How do people show prejudice?	What causes prejudice?	What does prejudice do to people? What happens when prejudice is or is not changed?
Jealousy, Anger? Hate? Competition?	How do people show jealousy? Anger? Hate? Competition?	What causes people to become jealous? Angry? Hateful? Competitive?	What happens to people when they become jealous? Angry? Hateful? Competitive?
Rebellion	How do people rebel?	Why do people rebel?	What happens when people rebel?
Success	What are some examples of success?	What causes success? Why do people want to become successful?	What happens when people do or do not achieve success? What does success do to people?
Liking/Disliking	What are some examples of people liking/disliking themselves?	What causes people to like/dislike themselves?	How do people show they like/dislike themselves?

(Continued)

THEME	EXAMPLES	CAUSES	EFFECTS
Disappoint-ment	How do people show disappointment? How do people act when they are disappointed?	What causes people to be disappointed?	What happens to people who are disappointed? What are the effects of being disappointed? How do people respond to disappointment?
Faking	How do people fake? Give examples of people not seeing the truth.	Why do people fake?	What are the effects of faking? What does faking do to the faker and the faked? What happens when a person pretends to be someone he/she isn't? (i.e. tough guy)
Happiness/Sadness	How do people show happiness or sadness?	What makes people happy or sad?	What does being happy or sad do to people?
Change	What are some examples of people changing? For the better? For the worse? What are some examples of people changing each other?	What makes people change? What keeps people from changing? How can another person make a person change for the better?	What are the effects of change? What happens when people can/cannot change?
Harm	What are some examples of people hurting each other?	Why do people hurt each other? What keeps people from hurting each other?	What are the effects of being hurt or hurting someone else?
Danger	What are some examples of danger that people face?	What are some causes of danger that people face? What causes people to respond to danger?	How do people respond to danger? What traits do characters show when responding to danger?
Fear	What are some examples of people being afraid?	What causes fear?	What are the effects of fear? What does fear cause?
Lying	What are some examples of people lying?	What causes people to lie?	What are the effects of people lying?
Courage	How do people show courage? What are some examples of people showing courage?	What causes people to show courage?	What are the effects of a person's courage? How does a person's courage affect his/her character?

(Continued)

THEME	EXAMPLES	CAUSES	EFFECTS
Freedom	What are some examples of freedom? How do people act when they are free?	What causes people to be free? What causes people to want freedom?	What are the effects of freedom? How do people respond to freedom?
Helping	How do people help each other?	Why do people help each other? Why do people need each other's help?	What happens when people help each other?
Choices	What are some choices that people make?	What causes people to make these choices?	What are the positive and negative effects of the choices made?
Determination/ Perseverance	How do people show determination and/or perseverance?	What causes people to show determination and/or perseverance?	What are the effects of a person's determination and/or perseverance?
Winning/Losing	What are some examples of people winning or losing?	What causes people to win or lose?	What are the effects of winning or losing? How do people act when they win or lose?
Revenge	How do people show revenge? How do people get back at each other?	What causes revenge?	What are the effects of revenge?
Ridicule	How do people make fun of each other?	Why do people laugh at each other?	What are the effects of people laughing at each other?
Trickery	How do people trick each other?	Why do people trick each other?	How does it make people feel to be tricked?
Criticism	How do people show criticism?	Why do people critize?	What happens when someone is criticized? What happens to other people?
Teasing	Where do people see lots of teasing?	Why do people tease?	What does teasing do to people?
Disagreement	Name some disagreements.	Why do people argue? Why do people disagree?	What happens to people when they disagree?
Blame	When do people blame each other?	Why do people blame things on each other?	What are the effects of blame?

(*Continued*)

THEME	EXAMPLES	CAUSES	EFFECTS
Mistakes	Name some mistakes people make.	Why do people make mistakes?	What happens when someone makes a mistake?
Fighting	Tell about some fights.	Why do people hit each other? Why do people fight? Why do people gang up?	What are the consequences of fighting?
Truth	What are some examples of truth?	Why do people not see the truth?	What happens when people do not see the truth?
Learning	Give examples of learning something.	What keeps people from learning something?	How do people feel when they cannot learn something?
Punishment	Tell about some punishments.	Why doesn't punishment always work?	What happens when someone punishes someone else?
Secrecy	What are some secrets?	How do secrets come out?	What happens when secrets come out?
Rumors	Give some examples of rumors.	How does a rumor start? How does a rumor spread?	What harm does spreading a rumor create? What happens when people go to another place? What happens when someone isn't fair?

THINKTRIX TOOLS FOR METACOGNITIVE DISCUSSION

Students respond well to visual and kinesthetic tools for metacognitive categorizing of questions, conversation, and text. These tools may be used for student response to the question, "What type(s) of thinking is/are required to answer this question or solve this problem?" or it can be asked, "What type of question is this?"

Magnetized cards with ThinkTrix symbols, or icons, and departure points can be moved around a white board. Each student can have a tool kit with a laminated matrix, small cards or pinch cards, and wheels displaying the thinking type icons. These, combined with the wall-cued One-Sided ThinkTrix, the Two-Sided ThinkTrix Discussion Board, the ThinkLink prototype shapes, and teacher/student constructed ThinkLinks, enable and encourage free-flowing classroom discourse.

When a teacher or a student asks a question, the other students can find the appropriate question type and can thereby be metacognitively active in the story discussion. Thus, all students become engaged thinkers regardless of whether they are asking or responding to a question.

Pinch Cards

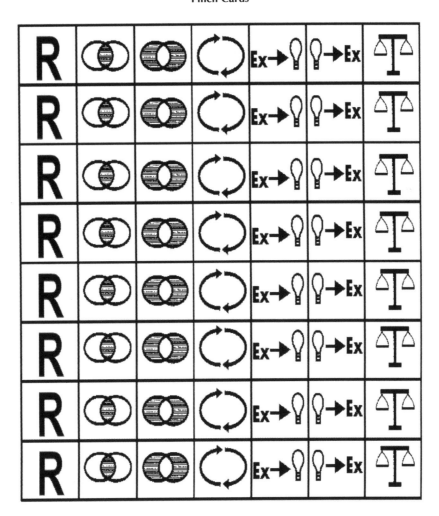

Wheels

The wheels can be used for individual students and as a large one for the wall or blackboar

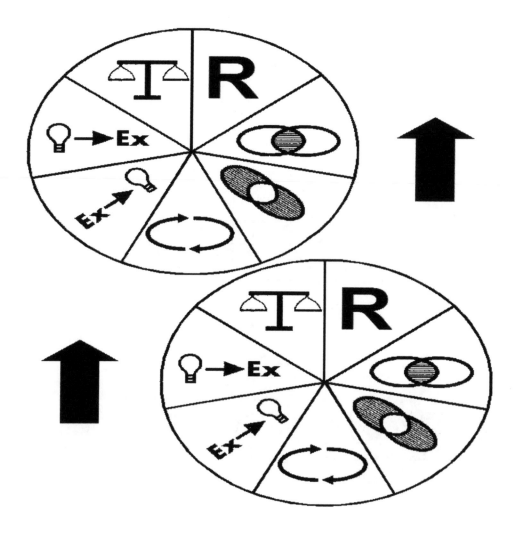

Question Generator

Students respond well to the structure of the Question Generator. They write a question in every box. Using this tool, they can ask and answer their own comprehension questions or classify questions from the text or test.

Topic: _____

R **Recall**

_____

Cause↔Effect

_____

Similarity

_____

Difference

_____

Ⓘ → Ex **Idea →Example(s)**

_____

Ex → Ⓘ **Example(s)→Idea(s)**

_____

Evaluation

_____

THE THINKLINK CLASSROOM: RESPONSE TO LITERATURE

The ThinkLink Classroom below uses supporting tools through which thought is shaped and understood. Students and the teacher create these tools and lists together.

A classroom geared to Response to Literature might include:

1. a large list of good to great books at several levels of difficulty.
2. wall-cued lists of books and stories known by most of the class.
3. wall-cued lists of characters from literature.
4. wall-cued and/or personal lists of traits/feelings and themes.
5. a wall-cued list of literary ideas/themes and/or character traits and/or feelings.
6. wall-cued ThinkLink shapes, or forms, as models.
7. wall-cued symbols, or icons, for thinking types.
8. wall-cued and/or personal set of ThinkTrix symbols, or icons, for thinking types.
9. a wall-cued list of literary ideas/themes and/or character traits and/or emotions.
10. individual wall-cued cards containing the ThinkTrix symbols, or icons.
11. wall-cued Think-Pair-Share variations for pair learning.
12. packets of suggested written activities that require responses at various levels of thought, complete with student written models.
13. a regimen of teacher's oral readings from great literature.
14. daily opportunities for silent reading.
15. lists of kinds of literature to create and/or craft skills to practice.
16. opportunities for students to "publish."
17. wall-cued lists or packets of questions that could be answered through literary allusion.
18. packets giving essay models (ThinkLinks to essay) to answer the questions.
19. designs for independent group interaction such as those in cooperative learning.
20. varied excerpts from great literature and from student writings, to be used as models.
21. teacher-student completed ThinkLinks displayed as models.
22. ongoing student produced *Big Idea* Cause/Effect ThinkLinks displayed around questions such as "How do people respond to danger?" "What are the causes/effects of friendship?"
23. a concentric, student-generated ThinkLink showing the positive effects of reading good books.
24. notebooks or journals in which written responses can be kept.
25. model lists of questions labeled by thinking types from the ThinkTrix matrix.
26. personal lists of good to great books at several levels of difficulty.
27. suggested activities that require responses at various levels of thinking, complete with models, written by students.
28. a collection of proverbs and expandable quotes.
29. a collection of original ideas and statements from the class—"published" and/or wall-cued.
30. opportunities for students to display their ThinkLinks and writing.
31. teacher- or student-displayed models of Cause/Effect essays.
32. student portfolios containing best ThinkLinks and writing.
33. designs for structured group interaction such as those in cooperative learning—Think-Pair-Share and Jig Saw, Numbered Heads, as well as other Kagan structures.

A Written Response to Literature might include:

1. excerpted models of great writing.
2. a collection of skeletal plots or story problems from various sources.
3. acting out or improvisation of scenes from literature.
4. a list or wheel of comprehension strategies such as visualizing, retelling, re-reading, and question formation.
5. a vocabulary program based on using words in multicontext.
6. an ongoing "book-selling" strategy in which students encourage each other to read.
7. a systematic way for oral reporting, in small groups, on books read.

8. a student-kept list of books read.
9. a list of effects of reading.
10. sets of multiple copies of books.
11. teacher-student or student-student conferencing strategy that encourages responses at different levels of thinking, as represented by the seven types of thinking on the ThinkTrix.
12. a collection of ThinkLink-charted samples of group and class discussions.
13. a regular homework assignment to read literature.
14. a learning center or wall cue containing a grid cell coded ThinkTrix enabling students to create their own questions.

Activities

CAUSE/EFFECT ESSAY MODEL

The Cause/Effect reasoning in composition form is a staple of education. The secret to success in teaching and motivation with the Cause/Effect essay is having worthwhile questions, metacognitive understanding, visual structures as with ThinkLinks, and models of writing. The following model of the entire process is effective in the intermediate grades.

IF ICHIRO COULD LEARN TO HIT LIKE THAT—YOU CAN LEARN TO THINK LIKE THIS

Learn to think by choosing a broad topic and

- wondering
- asking questions
- spreading out the questions
- hooking examples to the questions
- getting new questions from the examples
- choosing a question that you want to answer
- stating that question
- spreading out your answers
- hooking examples to the answer
- spreading out your examples
- hooking answers to the examples
- going from example to example connecting the answers that are the same

Topic Change
Figure A1

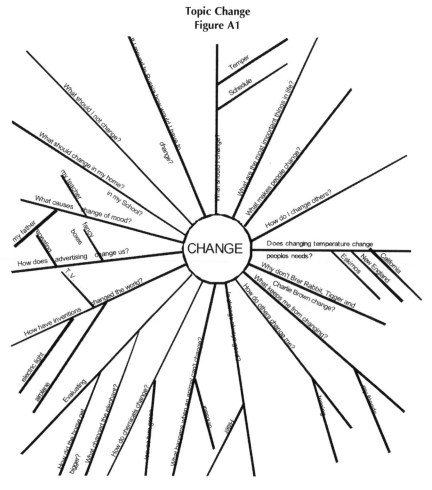

Specific Question Topic
Figure A2

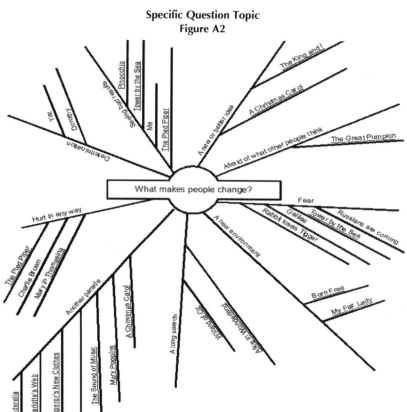

There are still questions that are more specific, narrower. For instance:

1. What makes people change for the better?
2. What makes people change for the worse?
3. How can fear change a person?
4. How can another person help a person change for the better?
5. How can another person help a person change for the worse?

How Can Another Person Make a Person Change for the Better?
Figure A3

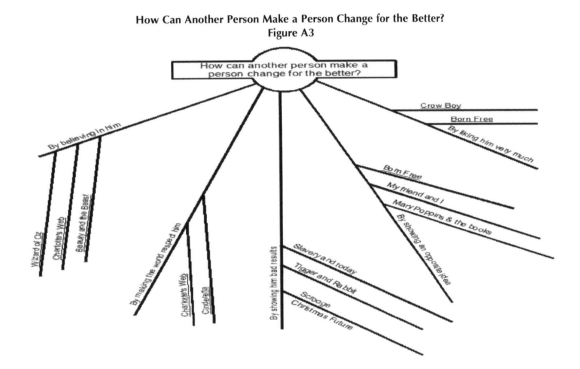

Or
How about another way to map that question?

How Can Another Person Help a Person Change for the Better?
Figure A4

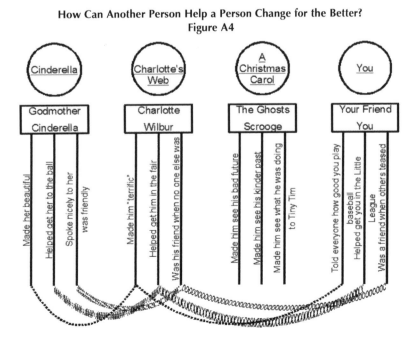

Connect the similar Causes. Color-code them.

Notice that Scrooge changes for different reasons. Could you find some people or characters that changed for the reasons that Scrooge changed? Make a new **ThinkLink** of examples like *A Christmas Carol*.

Now, let's change **Figure A4** to an outline: **How Can Another Person Help a Person Change for the Better?**

I.   Introduction
    A. What is "changing for the better?"
    B. The question
    C. Preview
       1. *Cinderella*
       2. *Charlotte's Web*
       3. You

II. Cinderella
    A. In the ashes
    B. Teased and taunted
    C. The Fairy Godmother
    D. The change
    E. The ball

III. Charlotte's Web
    A. Doomed and lonely pig
    B. No one cares
    C. Charlotte
    D. Radiant, terrific, some pig
    E. The Fair
    F. First Prize—Blue Ribbon
    G. New friends

IV. You
    A. New in school
    B. No one knows you, you hate everyone
    C. A boy plays ball with you
    D. You have a friend
    E. He tells everyone you can hit
    F. You are asked to come to Little League tryouts
    G. You make it
    H. You hate no one

V.   Connection Conclusion
    A. Changing what a person looks like
       1. Cinderella—a new gown
       2. Wilbur—radiant
       3. You—baseball player
    B. Helping a person go somewhere important
       1. Cinderella—the ball
       2. Wilbur—the Fair
       3. You—Little League tryouts
    C. Being a friend when no one else was
       1. Fairy Godmother
       2. Charlotte
       3. Your friend

Now, *The Essay*, straight from the outline: **How Can Another Person Help a Person Change for the Better?**

Some people change a lot, some almost never change. People can help each other change for the better, or worse. How do they help each other change for the better? To answer this question, let us look at *Cinderella, Charlotte's Web*, and a new boy in school.

Cinderella sits in the ashes and soot. The dust clogs her throat, and her sisters' teasing burns her ears. She does all the work and gets nothing but hate in return. She knows she is ugly, poor, and no good. This day, when her mean family leaves for the ball, she cries and cries. Through her tears she sees a glistening light and feels warmth. It is her Fairy Godmother. "Cinderella, look in the mirror. You are beautiful, rich, and the best girl in the world." Cinderella cannot believe it. She is radiant. She goes to the ball and floods goodness and beauty into all hearts, especially the Prince's. Her life is changed forever.

Wilbur is a runt, a pig doomed to an early ax. Fern saves him, but Wilbur finds loneliness in the barn almost as bad. No one cares for him. One morning he finds a small, thin friend, a spider named Charlotte. Charlotte cares about Wilbur and spins her care into magic words in her Web. Wilbur is saved. Everyone takes notice now of this miracle pig. He is "radiant," "some pig." Prize pigs go to the Fair and to the Fair he goes. With help from Charlotte and a nip in time from Templeton, he becomes a blue-ribbon pig. Charlotte dies, but three of her children stay with Wilbur, the happiest and longest-living pig in the barnyard.

"Hey, a new kid." The boy walks out to recess with everyone staring at him. He hates his school, new town, and the East. In California, he could play baseball most of the year. He stands by himself on the playground every day for a week. He cannot stand these kids.
"Hey kid, you wanta play catch?" The new kid throws slow at first and then burns them in. He wants Bowman's hands to hurt. "That kid can throw, watch him."
The boy's name is Bill, and his hands hurt, but he is with the new kid when they go into the building. Bill asks, "Where did you learn to throw hard like that?"
"In California."
"Can you hit?"
"I hit 400 in my California Little League."
"Whizzer, cool, wow!"
In one day, everyone knows the new kid's batting average, and five kids from different teams ask him to try out for their team. He tries out for Bill's team and makes it.
After the first game, the new kid doesn't stand by himself at recess any more. He doesn't hate school, or an icy town, or the East any more. In fact, things look almost as sunny as California.

One way to help a person change for the better is to change what he looks like. Cinderella switches her rags for a gown and no one sees any soot and ashes after that. Charlotte makes everyone think Wilbur is "terrific" and "radiant." Wilbur begins to feel that way himself. When the new kid first comes, he looks like anyone else, but after kids hear about his batting average, he looks different. They can practically see his muscles bulging.
Another way to help someone go from rags to riches is to help them go somewhere important. For instance, the Fairy Godmother sends Cinderella to the Prince's Ball, where she becomes the center of attention. A new Cinderella is born in the eyes of the guests. Charlotte's magic webs get Wilbur sent to the fair, where everyone can see the First Prize, Blue-Ribbon Pig. And finally, it is through Bill that the new kid is asked to Little League tryouts. There he proves himself.
A third way to help a person change for the better is to be his friend when no one else is. Loneliness is one big cause of unhappiness and even anger. Cinderella has no one in the world except her Fairy Godmother, who is her key to a new life of friends and happiness. Charlotte is, at first, Wilbur's only animal friend, but after a while everyone except Templeton likes him and even Templeton ends up helping him. If not for Bill, the new kid might miss Little League tryouts, because no one else takes the trouble to ask him about his baseball experience. The first friend opens the door to other friends, but without this first friend the door might have stayed closed for Cinderella, Wilbur, and the new kid.
To sum up, there are at least three ways another person can help a person change for the better: by changing what he looks like, by helping him go somewhere important, and by being his friend when he has no other friend.

CAUSE/EFFECT ESSAY SAMPLE: WHY DO PEOPLE FAKE?

The above model was used successfully to guide students in writing cause or effect essays. The teacher wrote and wall charted the first model, from theme to question to ThinkLink to outline to essay. A sixth-grade student in Lexington, Massachusetts followed the model and wrote the essay below.

Why Do People Fake?
Figure A5

The Wizard - Wizard of Oz	The People - The Emperor's New Clothes	The Owl - Winnie-the-Pooh
His neighbor's treatment made him seem wizardly.	The people were afraid of being told they were no good.	His neighbor's treatment made him seem smart.
The Wizard was afraid of a different future in Oz.	They were afraid of an unwanted future.	The Owl was afraid of a different future if he stopped.
He liked the idea of power.	They were afraid of losing their position in life.	He needed to keep up his reputation.

I. Introduction
    A. What is "faking?"
    B. Why do people fake?
    C. Review
       1. *Wizard of Oz*—the Wizard
       2. *The Emperor's New Clothes*—the people
       3. *Winnie-the-Pooh*—the Owl

II. *The Wonderful Wizard of Oz*—Wizard
    A. The Wizard lands and claims to be special.
    B. He lets himself become the Wizard.
    C. He can't get out of the office later.

III. *The Emperor's New Clothes*—people
    A. The Weavers make "cloth" for a new robe.
    B. The Emperor "sees" and believes.
    C. The people want to believe.

IV. *Winnie-the-Pooh*—Owl
    A. Pooh goes to Owl for writing help.
    B. The Owl writes imperfectly.
    C. It's accepted.

V. Connecting Conclusion
    A. His neighbors' treatment
       1. Wizard—made him seem smart and wizardly
       2. Owl—made him seem smart
    B. To keep up the reputation
       1. Wizard—acted as a powerful wizard
       2. People—their jobs and positions
       3. Owl—as a smart owl
    C. Like the idea of power
       1. Wizard—from not being Wizard and powerful
       2. People—from not "seeing" the clothes
       3. Owl—as being smarter than the rest

WHY DO PEOPLE FAKE?

Some people need to fake. Some like to for fun, at first, but then when they want to stop, they can't stop faking. Others are forced into a faking position. Pretending to be something you aren't is, in my opinion, a handicap. You will see this in the following situations: Owl in *Winnie the Pooh*, "Eeyore's Birthday"; the people in *The Emperor's New Clothes*; and the Wizard in *The Wizard of Oz*.

"Eeyore's Birthday"—Pooh knows it's Eeyore's birthday and feels the need to get him a present. So he thought and thought. "Ah, I have it. I'll give him a pot of honey." On the way to Eeyore's, Pooh starts to get hungrier and hungrier and so starts eating the honey little by little until it's all gone. "Oh dear, I've eaten Eeyore's birthday present. But it's a nice jar. I could still give it to him. He could use it for something. I know, I'll go to Owl for a message for my jar." At Owl's house, "Knock, knock!" "Would you write, 'Happy birthday, Eeyore' on this jar? You know it's his birthday." "Oh! It is? I didn't know that. O.K., now let me see." He thought. "Well, I guess it's RAPPL BARITHADAY." And that's what he wrote. "Thank you, Owl." "It's nothing."

Emperor's New Clothes—The Emperor loves his clothes. Two weavers come to him with a proposition that they will weave for him the finest clothes for a ghastly amount. He accepts this offer, and so the clothes are made. "Behold, the Emperor comes to show his new clothes. Whoever does not see them is proclaimed a fool." "Oh! Aren't they lovely?" "Yes, gorgeous." "They're made of silk with gold woven into them." "Ah, oh, ya, a silk with, ah, gold woven into them." So, the Emperor's wish of having the grandest clothes has come true.

The Wonderful Wizard of Oz—Note: This question is being asked before the actual story. The Wizard's balloon lands in a mysterious place called Oz. The people, the Munchkins, that is, think him such a grand and glorious person with a very advanced machine, his balloon. The Munchkins think him very great and made him the Wizard of Oz. "Hoorah" "Hoorah" "Hoorah for our new Wizard. Hip, hip, hoorah. Hip, hip, Hoorah." "Why thank you, thank you. I don't know what to say." And so he became the Wizard of Oz.

One reason that people might fake would be because of their neighbors' treatment of them, such as in *The Wonderful Wizard of Oz*. The Munchkins forced him into Wa faking position by proclaiming him Wizard. In the story "Eeyore's Birthday," and in other stories, Owl was asked for writing, which no one could give. So, Owl pretended he could, and his neighbors trusted him and kept asking him for writing, and so this became a habit of his.

Another reason for Owl's behavior would be that he wanted to keep up the reputation of his ancestors, owls, being smart. This can also be found in *The Emperor's New Clothes*, using reputations as referring to the people's jobs, where the people, if they lost their reputations, would lose their jobs and positions.

Some people fake for the reason that they like some power. Owl saw his chance for power by being "seemingly smarter" than the rest. The Wizard saw his chance for power by the fact that he was a "Wizard."

The fourth reason that I will discuss for faking is that they were afraid of an unwanted future after they had started faking and finally wanted to stop. Owl was afraid of not being "smart." The Emperor's people were afraid of losing their jobs and the Wizard of just not being a wizard.

So, there you have it. Four of the main reasons for faking are the neighbors' treatment, wanting to keep up their reputations, liking the idea of power, and being afraid of an unwanted future.

RESPONSE TO LITERATURE ACTIVITIES

Every teacher should have a set of activities that could be used at any time with students. The following activities enable students to respond to literature by relating it to their lives, other literature, film, or drama. Some responses may be most appropriately written in journals or shown as a ThinkLink.

1. In the story, list in order the important choices that a character has to make. Show on a ThinkLink the causes of making the choices and/or the causes that make it difficult to make the choices. For example, Mafatu saves Uri because he loves him. It is hard to make the choice because he is so afraid of the sea.
2. Show on a ThinkLink the effects of making the choice. For example, some of the effects of Mafatu's choice to leave the island include conquering the storm, killing a shark, and killing a boar. What type of thinking are you doing?

3. What is the most important choice made in the story? Why? Show your thinking on a ThinkLink and label on the ThinkLink the types of thinking you are doing.

4. List some choices you have made in your life. Find choices made by characters from stories that are like choices you made. Explain why the choice is similar to your choice. Does it have similar causes? Does it have similar effects? Can you make a ThinkLink before you write?

5. In what ways are you similar to a character in the story you are reading? Show on a Venn Diagram ThinkLink similar traits/feelings, problems/solutions, or choices.

6. Find several characters in any of the stories you have read and who are most like you. Explain how you are similar to them. Which one is most similar? Explain to a partner before you write. Discuss the types of thinking you are doing.

7. Select several characters from other stories you think are most like a character in the story. Show on a ThinkLink how they are similar to the character. Which one is most similar to the character? In what way?

8. Make up a question for your partner for which you have the answer. For example, how is Cricket like Charlotte? Ask your partner to type the thinking using the ThinkTrix types.

9. Compare choices from the story you are reading with choices from other stories. What type of thinking are you doing? Show the similarities and differences on a ThinkLink before you write.

10. Themes such as fear, courage, honor or insult, success, saving or overcoming are ideas that run through a story. Discover themes by first finding similar or related events from the story. Connect the themes to these supporting events with a ThinkLink.

11. What is the main or most important theme of the story? Why do you think so? Discuss with a partner and/or write from the ThinkLink. What types of thinking are you doing?

12. Show how themes in the story connect by creating a ThinkLink shape. For example, Mafatu overcomes fear and insult through courage. He saves his own honor through his success.

13. Compare the theme in the story you are reading with the same theme from another story. For example, saving in *The Wizard of Oz* is like saving in *Charlotte's Web* because Dorothy and Charlotte save the Lion and Wilbur from feeling insecure. They make them proud of themselves. Saving in *Call It Courage* is not like saving in *Pinocchio* because Mafatu saves himself, and Pinocchio gets help from Geppetto and Cricket. Create a ThinkLink shape to show your answer.

14. Create a skeletal plot for the story by listing the most important events in order. Choose a ThinkLink shape such as Story Steps or Mountain Diagram to reveal the plot. Include the problem, choices, conflict, solutions, and conclusion.

15. Choose another story, a Mother Goose tale, an Aesop Fable, or a fairy tale that has a similar skeletal plot to that of your story. Create a ThinkLink showing the main events of this plot and prove it is similar by connecting these events to those in your story.

16. Every story has a problem. What is the main problem in the story? How is it solved or not solved? Find other stories that have a similar problem. Create a ThinkLink to show the similarities. Choose a main problem from one of the stories on the list. With other students act out the scene where it is solved.

17. Select several stories and find how they are in any way similar to your story by comparing causes, effects, choices, events, characters, and/or main themes. Choose a ThinkLink shape, such as a web or concentric circle, to show these similarities.

18. We are all characters in our own life story. Choose a story from the list that reminds you in some way of your family. How are the characters in the story similar to you and members of your family? How are they different? Write your answer or create a ThinkLink to compare.

19. Re-create in writing a scene from a book, a novel, a story, a movie, a play, or your life.

20. With a partner select a dramatic scene from a favorite story and act it out for another pair of students. Discuss the scene afterward asking about the causes and effects of the action in the scene.

21. From your portfolio select a ThinkLink you have completed and use it as a blueprint to answer the ThinkLink's question in writing.

22. Create ratios:

Figure A6

$$\frac{\text{Charlotte}}{\text{Wilbur}} = \frac{\text{Dorothy}}{\text{Tinman}} = \frac{\text{Cricket}}{\text{Pinocchio}} = \frac{\text{Mafatu}}{\text{Uri}} = \frac{\text{Leslie}}{\text{Jess}} = \frac{\text{Helpers}}{\text{Helped}}$$

Glossary of Terms

Anatomy of knowledge—the visual shapes that hold knowledge in place and in some Relationship to **ThinkLinks**

Architecture of knowledge—the basic **types** of thinking that organize and generate knowledge

Blueprint—a **ThinkLink** used as an outline, or organizer, for written composition

Coding—symbols used in place of words on **ThinkLinks**

Cognitive drift—a state of confusion that exists when students and/or teachers are unclear as to what type of thinking is being asked; a mutual misunderstanding due to a lack of connection between the general and the specific

Cognitive mapping—a generic term for the shaping of thought; synonymous in general with creating a **ThinkLink**

Concept Web—a **ThinkLink** that features a feeling or character trait derived from character analysis

Cooperative learning—the structured interaction between and among students in the service of learning and relationship building. Examples are **Think-Pair-Share** and the Kagan activities and structures.

Cues—written, verbal, manipulative, and hand signal reminders of what to do, how to think, and what is known

Demonstration and Guided Practice and Independent Production—two stages of instruction

Event—one or more occurrences in life or literature; a concrete happening that can be used to derive or support an idea or generalization

Example—an event or object from which ideas can be derived or to which ideas can be connected

Feeling—a classification for an emotion

Focal Points—**Character, Event, Theme, Story**, and other concepts on the **ThinkTrix** that are points of departure for thinking. These four terms are also the names of the **Kinds of ThinkLinks** demonstrated in this book.

Forms—varying shapes of a **ThinkLink** such as a web, wheels, jellyfish, triangle, etc.

Idea—concept, trait, theme, or generalization; an abstraction

Instructional stages—Demonstration and Guided Practice and Independent Production are instructional phases for teaching in the **ThinkLink Classroom**

Instructional tool—any device, chart, comprehensive reminder, template, or list that facilitates classroom learning and teaching

Literature—novels, short stories, fairy tales, fables, poetry, and other reading contexts

Literature journal—a student notebook for responding to literature

Metacognition—knowing how you know; knowledge of the workings of the mind

Metacognitive mapping—the creating and using of cognitive mapping, or **ThinkLinks**, when considering the **type{s}** of thinking involved, as identified on the **ThinkTrix** typology

97

Me Web—a **ThinkLink** with the student as the focal point

Modified ThinkTrix—the metacognitive framework used as an organizer of this book

One-sided ThinkTrix—an enlarged **ThinkTrix** matrix in which the grid cells are coded as 1a, 1b, 2f, and so forth, allowing for easy identification of thinking types

Pair Talk—a basic cooperative learning framework in which partners discuss in free or structured ways

Prototype—a format; a **ThinkLink** shape, form, or design coupled with the thinking type(s) and focal point involved; a blank model

Question–response cues—the **ThinkTrix** thinking **types** displayed on the matrix or individually, which can also be prompted verbally or with hand signals

Response prompts—questions or statements in various **types** of thinking designed to elicit responses

Samples—actual examples of completed **ThinkLinks**

Skeletal ThinkLink—a partially developed **ThinkLink** for students to complete

Story Element—plot, setting, problem/solution, characterization, event, theme

Theme—a recurring idea; a "thread" running through a story or composition

The ThinkLink Classroom—the environment within which the **ThinkLink** metacognitive mapping strategy operates together with the allied activities and methods

ThinkLink—a metacognitive map of thinking

ThinkLink kind—a classification for **ThinkLink** in which **Character, Event, Theme**, and **Story** are points of departure for thinking

Thinking types—basic actions of the mind, or classifications of the basic acts of thinking such as: Recall, Cause/Effect, Similarity, Difference, Idea→Example(s), Example(s)→Idea(s), and Evaluation

ThinkLink typing—student labeling of **ThinkLinks** according to the **types** of thinking being used

Think-Pair-Share—a question–response cooperative learning structure in which **Think Time**, or **Wait Time**, is given after a question or task. Students are cued to discuss or work with a partner, and responses are sometimes shared with the larger group. Students do not raise hands or **Pair** until the teacher or leader cues them to do so. The teacher has the option of skipping the **Pair Mode** or **the Share Mode**.

ThinkTrix—a matrix with thinking **types** on one axis and points of departure on the other axis; a basic and accessible metacognitive typology; one-sided

ThinkTrix Discussion Board: Two-Sided Matrix—a cooperative discussion tool allowing students to use the **ThinkTrix** from opposite sides

Thought process—thinking that incorporates more than one thinking **type**; complex thinking such as problem-solving, decision-making, inquiring, and creating

Trait—a classification for an often-repeated pattern of behavior that may change, or evolve, or not

Variation—a sub category of a **ThinkLink** variety such as shape, color, symbol coding systems, and artistic embellishments

Variety—a subcategory of a kind of **ThinkLink**

Wait Time—the period of time between the teacher and the student's question and the first person who responds. This interval should be at least three seconds. This is known as **Wait Time I. Wait Time II** is the time interval between the student's response and the response of the next speaker, teacher, or student. **Wait Time**, or **Think Time**, can only be achieved if hands are raised on a cue from the teacher or leader.

Writing samples—student work samples created in combination with the **ThinkLink** metacognitive mapping strategy

ThinkTrix Bibliography

The ThinkTrix Bibliography is a reminder that this metacognitive typology has been thoroughly field-tested.

Adger, Carolyn; Kalyanpur, Maya; Peterson, Dana; and Bridger, Teresa. 1995. *Engaging Students: Thinking, Talking, Cooperating.* Thousand Oaks, CA: Corwin Press.

Arends, Richard, I. 1997. *Classroom Instruction and Management.* Boston, MA: McGraw-Hill. 224–226.

Beyer, Barry, K. 1997. *Improving Student Thinking: A Comprehensive Approach.* Boston, MA: Allyn and Bacon. 24–25.

Bridger, Teresa. 1990. *A Scenario for the implementation of the question/ response cues for special education students.* **Unpublished Paper**.

Bridger, Teresa. 1996. *The use of ThinkTrix as a questioning strategy for teaching of high school students identified with learning disabilities.* **Doctoral Dissertation**. Fairfax, VA: George Mason University.

Carlton, Stephanie. 1992–1993. *Critical Thinking Year Two.* **Curriculum Guide**. Richmond, VA: Henrico City Public School System. 77–105.

Carroll, Kathleen. 2000. *Science for Every Learner: Brain-Compatible Pathways to Scientific Literacy.* Tuscon, AZ: Zephyr Press. Introduction, xiii.

Carroll, Kathleen. 2007. *A Guide to Great Field Trips.* Chicago, IL: Zephyr Press. 122–127, 163–166, 175.

Carter, Carol and Kravits, Sarah Lyman. 1996. *How to Achieve Your Goals.* **Keys to Success**. Upper Saddle River, NJ: Prentice-Hall, Second edition. 124–128.

Carter, Carol; Bishop, J.; and Kravits, Sarah Lyman. 2006. *Success instructional manual to accompany.* **Keys to Success**. Upper Saddle River, NJ: Pearson Education, Inc. 297–302.

Coley, Joan D. and DePinto, Thommie. 1988. *Merging reciprocal teaching question/ response cues.* **Unpublished Paper**.

Coley, Joan D. and DePinto, Thommie. 1989. *Reciprocal teaching: theme and variations.* **Unpublished Paper**.

Coley, Joan D. and Hoffman, Dianne M. 1990. *Overcoming learned helplessness in at-risk readers.* **Journal of Reading**. April, 497–502.

Coley, Joan J. D.; Craig, Sharon; DePinto, Thommie; and Gardiner, Rosalie. 1993. *From college to classroom: Three teachers' accounts of their adaptations of reciprocal teaching.* **Elementary School Journal**. Chicago, IL: University of Chicago Press. Vol. 94, No. 2, 256–266.

Craig, Sharon; DePinto, Thommie; Gardiner, R.; Marks, M.; and Pressley, M. 1993. *Three teachers' adaptations of reciprocal teaching in comparison to traditional reciprocal teaching.* **Elementary School Journal**. University of Chicago Press. Vol. 94, No. 2, 267–283.

DePinto, Thommie. 1986. *Listening to children's voices.* **Unpublished Paper**.

DePinto, Thommie. 1987. *The extension of thinking skills in comprehension.* **Unpublished Paper**.

DePinto, Thommie. 1988. *Action research: A teacher's perspective.* **Reading: Issues and Practices 5**. Westminster, MD. Spring.

English, Evelyn. 1999. *Gift of Literacy for the Multiple Intelligence Classroom.* Arlington Heights, IL: Skylight Publishers, Inc. 144–146.

Forte, Imogene and Schurr, Sandra. 1993. *The Definitive Middle School Guide.* Nashville, TN: Incentive Publications. 217.

Foster, Karen K. 2006. *Spin the wheel of thinking to activate critical thought.* **IRA: Journal of Content Area Reading**. University of central Missouri. Vol. 5, No. 1, 67–79.

Hattie, John. 2009. *Visible Learning: A Synthesis of Over 800 Meta-Analyses Relating to Achievement.* New York, NY: Routledge.

Hoffman, Barbara. 1987. *Thirty-four Years Later.* **The Early Adolescence Magazine**. Vol. 1, No. 4, 6–9.

Keeling, Janet, Editor. 1993. *The Middle School Guide.* Nashville, TN: Incentive Publications, Inc. 24–25.

King, Alison. 1992. *Facilitating elaborative learning through guided student-generated questioning.* **Educational Psychiatrist**. Vol. 27, No. 1, 111–126.

Knight, Janice E. 1990. *Coding journal entries.* **Journal of Reading**. Vol. 34, No. 1, 42–47.

Koza, Nancy. 1990. *A Scenario for the implementation for the ThinkTrix at the primary level.* **ThinkTrix Tools to Teach 7 Essential Thinking Skills**. 22–25, 109.

Lyman, Frank T. 1987. *The ThinkTrix: A classroom tool for thinking in response to reading.* **Reading: Issues and Practices, Yearbook of the State of Maryland International Reading Association Council**. Vol. 4, 15–18.

Lyman, Frank T. 1992. *Think-Pair-Share, ThinkTrix, THINKLINKS, and weird facts: Interactive system for cooperative thinking.* **Enhancing Thinking Through Cooperative Learning**. Edited by Neil Davidson and Toni Worsham. Columbia University, NY: Teachers College Press. 169–182.

Lyman, Frank T.; Koza, Nancy; and McKnight, Mary. 1993. *Every-Student- Response through transactional signaling: Cooperative cues for cooperative thinking.* **Cooperative Learning**. California, CA: Cooperative Learning Press. Vol. 13, No. 2.

Lyman, Frank T. 1994. *Cooperative learning and every-student-response: Their essential relationship.* **MAACIE Newsletter, February 1994**. MD: MAACIE Newsletter. Vol. 7(3).

Lyman, Frank T. 1995. *Clarity and cooperative learning: The concrete-abstract connection.* **MAACIE Newsletter Nov./Dec. 1995**. Columbia, MD: MAACIE Newsletter.

Lyman, Frank T. and Rogers-Newman, Shirley. 1996. *Building philosophical foundations: The ThinkTrix model in the classroom.* **Bookbird**. Vol. 34, No. 3. Fall.

Lyman, Frank T. 1996. *The teaching of the uses of the ThinkTrix.* Carter, Carol and Kravits, Sarah Lyman. Supplement to the Instructional Manual of **Keys to Success**. Upper Saddle River, NJ: Prentice Hall.

Lyman, Frank T. 1996. *Independent and cooperative interpretation of thinking prompts: learning to translate performance-based tasks through the ThinkTrix.* **MAACIE Newsletter Fall 1996**. Columbia, MD: MAACIE Newsletter.

Lyman, Frank T. 2005. **ThinkTrix, the Smart Card**. San Clemente, CA: Kagan Publishing.

Lyman, Frank T. 2016. **ThinkTrix; Tools to Teach 7 Essential Thinking Skills**. San Clemente, CA. Kagan Publishing, First edition.

Marzano, Robert, J., et al. 2001. *Classroom Instruction that Works*. Alexandria, VA: Association for Supervision and Curriculum Development.

McTighe, Jay and Lyman, Frank T. 1989. *Cueing thinking in the classroom: The promise of theory-embedded tools.* **Educational Leadership**. April. Alexandria, VA: ASCD. 18–24.

McTighe, Jay and Lyman, Frank T. 1992. *Mind tools for matters of the mind.* **If Minds Matter, A Forward to the Future**. Vol. II. Edited by Costa, Arthur; Bellanca, James; and Fogerty, Robin. Palatine, IL: Skylight Publishing, Inc. 71–90.

Polack, Sam. 1989. *The continuum within each thinking type: The third dimension.* **ThinkTrix Tools to Teach 7 Essential Thinking Skills**. 48–52.

Piercy-DePinto, Thommie. 1997. *The effects of multi-strategy instruction as measured by a standardized assessment of reading comprehension.* **Doctoral Dissertation**. College Park, MD: University of Maryland.

Ransom, Kathryn; Roettger, Doris; and Staplin, Phyllis, Project Coordinators. 1995. *Reading Assessment in Practice-Book of Readings & Video Tapes*. IRA. Appendix E.

Rogers, Shirley. 1990. *Applications and scenarios for the implementation of ThinkTrix in intermediate grades: Social studies/language arts.* **Unpublished Paper**.

Solomon, Richard and Solomon, Elaine. 1995. *Handbook for the fourth R: Relationship Activities for Cooperative & Collegial learning*. Columbia, MD: Richard Solomon Publisher. Chapters 6 & 7.

Stiggins, Richard; Arter, Judith; Chappuis, Jan; and Chappuis, Stephen. 2005. **Classroom Assessment for Student Learning**. Portland, OR: Assessment Training Institute. 267–269.

Valencia, Sheila; Hiebert, E.; and Afflerbach, Peter. 1994. *User's Handbook*. **Authentic Reading Assessment Practices and Possibilities**. Newark, DE: IRA. Appendix E.

Willis, Judy, M. D. 2008. *Teaching the Brain to Read: Strategies for Improving Fluency, Vocabulary, and Comprehension*. Alexandria, VA: Association for Supervision and Curriculum Development.

Winebrenner, Susan and Dina Brulles. 2008. *The Cluster Grouping Handbook: How to Challenge Gifted Students and Improve Achievement for All*. Minneapolis, MN: Free Spirit Publishing. 138–140.

Winebrenner, Susan and Dina Brulles. 2012. *Teaching Gifted Kids in Today's Classroom: Strategies and Techniques Every Teacher Can Use*. Minneapolis, MN: Free Spirit Publishing. 157–160.

Winebrenner, Susan. 2014. *Teaching Kids with Learning Difficulties in the Regular Classroom*. Minneapolis, MN: Free Spirit Publishing, Third edition. 69–70.

About the Authors

Frank T. Lyman Jr. has been an influential teacher educator since 1960. His outstanding contributions have been in teacher education as well as in classroom teaching in K–12. Very few educators have had the impact he has had on the daily practice of American teachers. Publication of this book has long been a goal, and he says that he owes this publication to his co-authors and the many teachers who have pushed him for years to write. He insists that without these colleagues and students with whom he has learned so much, he would not have been able to organize his strategies, or even have thought of them in the first place.

Frank taught elementary school for eleven years and student teachers K–12 for the University of Maryland, College Park and the Howard County Public School System as the Coordinator of the Teacher Education Center for twenty-six years. He taught undergraduate courses, given hundreds of workshops and seminars, and taught thirty-five graduate courses in teacher education. He received his Masters Degree in Education at Harvard University in 1960. He then taught in Montgomery County, Maryland, for two years, and in team teaching schools in Lexington, Massachusetts and in Howard County, Maryland, from 1962 to 1970. He currently is an educational writer, and consultant. His most recent endeavor in teacher education is with the University of California, Berkeley, and the University of Maryland, Baltimore County, in School Leadership.

Though he is nationally and internationally recognized for educational innovations such as Think-Pair-Share and ThinkTrix, he is most respected by the students and colleagues who know him best as a motivating and influential teacher. Along with humor and a spontaneous inventiveness, his signature in teaching is his ability to teach as he recommends that others teach—as close to the state-of-the-art as possible. That is, his medium is his message. He has developed with student teachers, graduate students, teachers, and university colleagues several theory practice templates, including *The B Wheel* and a widely used heuristic called *The Problem Solving-Action Research Flowchart*.

In 1965, the epiphany of ThinkLinks changed his teaching forever. Though he gave several workshops in the Boston area on the uses of diagramming of thinking, he never wrote on the subject or even put his name on the handouts. The field-testing in Lexington was impressive, but became more extensive in Maryland among teachers and University of Maryland researchers. It was in Howard County, Maryland, with several teachers and co-authors, Arlene Mindus and Charlene López, that ThinkLinks became established and developed from 1970 to 1990. Other Maryland counties also became involved and, of course, variations on the basic idea of cognitive mapping found other genesis points and other labels nationally and in England.

The ThinkLinks with ThinkTrix book exposes the thinking that underlies cognitive mapping and is written in such a way that clarifies for teachers the anatomy of the strategy. The accessible typology of the ThinkTrix makes possible a shared metacognition in the classroom that most graphic organizer strategies do not. What Frank Lyman and his colleagues hope for is nothing less than the enfranchisement of student minds through the shaping and understanding of thought.

Frank Lyman is a graduate of Haverford College and has a doctorate in Administration, Supervision, and Curriculum from the University of Maryland, College Park. His recognitions include the Maryland Association of Teacher Education's *Maryland Educator of the Year Award*, the National Association of Teacher Education's *Clinician of the Year Award*, the Maryland Association for Supervision and Curriculum Development's *Judith Ruchkin Research Award*, the University of Maryland's *Presidential Award for Outstanding Service to the Schools*, Kappa Delta Pi's *Outstanding Educator of the Year Award* by undergraduate students at the University of Maryland, and the University of Maryland's College of Education's *Alumni Award for the Outstanding Professional*.

Charlene López was a dedicated, innovative teacher of primary grade elementary students for thirty four years. She centered her class discourse on children's literature, poetry, and writing. Through the use of ThinkLinks with ThinkTrix, Charlene solved the problem of the excessive amount of teacher talk and teacher direction in group and class discussions.

Charlene's greatest accomplishment as an elementary classroom teacher was being an integral part of the students' learning experience by instilling a love and enthusiasm for learning, building confidence and self worth, and emphasizing strengths and talents. She provided a rich and stimulating learning environment, engaging students' curiosity, independent thinking, and questioning. She challenged them to reach their highest potential, and took pride in their creative ideas and written products. She always set high expectations and standards for her students' performance and achievement where they worked cooperatively and celebrated one another's efforts and accomplishments.

In this dynamic, interactive environment, her students had a significant and influential role as critical thinkers and learners in response to literature, reading selections, prose, poetry, and writing. Charlene's lessons connected and linked learning by using an enthusiastic questioning strategy as well as modeling, so that students understood where they had been, where they were, and where they were going in the hierarchy of the curriculum.

In selecting a topic for her master's thesis in the mid-1970s, Charlene realized that Frank Lyman's ThinkLinks could be employed as an effective means of immersing her students in a more dynamic verbal interaction to produce comparative, divergent, and convergent relationships in the thinking and reading process. Her topic, *Classroom Application and Assessment of the Use of Diagramming in the Reading Program*, included planned ThinkLinks with ThinkTrix activities as a structured medium to allow students to anchor new ideas to their already present cognitive structure. It gave them a way to thoughtfully organize and purposefully seek new ideas. The building and transferring of knowledge was fostered through the thinking process of the **ThinkLink** strategy. It encouraged them to become more prolific, creative, and critical in their understanding and response to literature, offering the framework within which the thinking took place, the missing link between creative thinking and structure needed for them to think at higher levels. ThinkLinks were the products that displayed their creative and productive thinking.

In the area of visual organization, Charlene was perhaps the most accomplished teacher in the country. In 1972, she definitely was one of the first three teachers in Maryland to make comprehensive use of ThinkLinks with what was later to become known as ThinkTrix as a means for students to generate and organize thought. Charlene and her students were the pioneers. Her students led circle discussions with their own questions and responses, in which they listened critically, evaluated, and responded to each other, ultimately leading to a respect for each other's ideas. An appreciation and love of books and literature increased as they discussed character traits/feelings, and "change of character." They acquired empathy and understanding of the characters, analyzed story plots, understood problems, solutions, conflicts, themes, and important choices made by the characters. As a result, the **ThinkLink** process became the centerpiece of her highly effective language arts program.

One of the original proponents of pair learning, Charlene gave students the opportunity to work with study partners as they learned cooperatively. Student lists of traits/feelings and themes, class ThinkLinks displayed around the classroom, *Idea Books, Response Journals*, ThinkTrix pinch cards used to generate students' questions for group discussions, *Types of Thinking* as models of questions, and personal paperback novels for students to identify traits/feelings, themes, problems, solutions, and choices were some of the cooperative learning materials Charlene created and used in her classroom.

Much of Charlene's success with her students was due to an instinctive gift that enabled her to reach into their lives and find their potential for success. She bonded with each student in a special, personal way. They were inspired to want to learn and given the confidence to know that they could do the job well. Students were eager and assured that their efforts would be successful and recognized. Charlene was a master of meaningful praise. Her enthusiasm was transmitted to her students, and her classes had consistently been were marked with a love for learning.

Charlene's inspired teaching and caring for children was recognized formally in 1987 when she was Howard County's first elementary school teacher to receive the prestigious *Washington Post's Agnes Meyer Excellence in Teaching Award*. Along with her inventiveness and high standards, she was recognized for her absolute dedication to children and their education. This recognition was well deserved, as she chose to work with elementary students of all academic levels and diverse demographic circumstances. Students and parents benefited for three decades from a great American classroom teacher—an inspiration and model to numerous teachers and administrators. Her success was emblematic of the best the profession had to offer in intellect, compassion, vision, and skill.

Charlene is a graduate of the University of Texas, Austin, and has a Master's Degree in Elementary Education from the University of Maryland, College Park.

Arlene Mindus exhibited great energy and productivity throughout thirty-seven years in public education as a classroom teacher, university supervisor, team leader, assistant principal, and a principal before retiring in 2004. Her friendly, loving, open attitude and manner were the foundation of her success as a teacher and administrator.

Arlene worked with Frank Lyman in his capacity as the coordinator of the Teacher Education Center for the University of Maryland, College Park, and the Howard County Public School System for twenty years. Not only did she have a thorough knowledge of instructional strategy, but she was also a pioneer in cooperative learning and the teaching of thinking. In 1976, she was co-inventor with Frank Lyman of Think-Pair-Share, a technique involving all students in classroom discussion and probably the most used cooperative learning technique in the country. In addition, she was one of the first teachers in the country to use ThinkLinks, or graphic organizers, a strategy for the creation and organization of thought now in worldwide use along with ThinkTrix, a matrix with thinking types on one axis and points of departure on the other axis.

Arlene was creative, always positive, and a child advocate. She was a proponent of the arts and all forms of creativity. She practiced and promoted a blending of form and content, of creativity within structure. Her sense of humor helped to create a climate of warmth around her. Students and adults alike were encouraged to have fun and take risks.

As a classroom teacher, she excelled in teaching students how to express themselves well in writing and how to appreciate literature and poetry. She developed many cooperative-learning strategies to assist them in becoming proficient in expressing their thoughts in writing. Students in her classrooms benefited from her positive feedback and reinforcement regarding their potential to be successful as writers and readers. Over two thousand students were positively affected by their contact with Arlene, who was always a favorite teacher with students and their parents. Few teachers were as successful in motivating students to develop their full potential while recognizing that they were both lovable and capable as individuals.

Some of her success as an administrator was based upon her experience as a university cooperating teacher, mentoring twenty-five student teachers and successful with each and every one. As these student teachers established their own **ThinkLink** classrooms after accepting teaching positions throughout the country, ThinkLinks with ThinkTrix were becoming standard teaching practices with cooperative learning.

The University of Maryland recognized Arlene as one of eleven Master Teachers statewide as part of their three-year federally funded *Clinical Classroom Project*. She worked with teachers throughout Maryland, and her classroom was used as a model for ThinkLinks with ThinkTrix. This was another foundation block of her work as a school administrator. She had a firm grasp of the elements of best practices.

Arlene has been a lifelong learner. She consistently improved her knowledge of teaching, of administration, and of children's needs. It seemed that no learning opportunity was ever dismissed without evaluating its potential for improving the lives of the students and teachers in her schools. She was an instructional leader whose focus was and always had been on motivating and enabling others to learn and do their best. She led, not by checklists, numbers, and fear, but by example and expertise. Arlene was a positive role model for many teachers and prospective teachers, and she made an unusually great commitment to teaching and education. She was a teacher and administrator that children never forget.

Arlene is a graduate of Framingham State University, has a Master's Degree in Administration, Supervision, and Curriculum from the University of Maryland, College Park, an Advanced Professional Certificate in Administration, Supervision, and Curriculum from the Maryland State Department of Education, and received her National Principal Mentoring Certification from the National Association of Elementary School Principals. She was a participant in Harvard University's Principals' Center Summer Institute, *Leadership: An Evolving Vision*. She was the recipient of Framingham State University's *Outstanding Achievement Award*, Maryland Association of Teacher Educators' *Outstanding Supervising Teacher Award*, and the prestigious *Washington Post*'s *Distinguished Educational Leadership Award*, and she was listed in *Who's Who In American Education*.

Made in the USA
Middletown, DE
30 December 2017